~The Official~ Bar Guide to DARTS

Patrick Chaplin, PhD, darts historian

PUZZLE WRIGHT PRESS

An imprint of Sterling Publishing Co., Inc.

www.puzzlewright.com

TO MAUREEN

Puzzlewright Press and the distinctive Puzzlewright Press logo are registered trademarks of Sterling Publishing Co., Inc.

Library of Congress Cataloging-in-Publication Data

Chaplin, Patrick.
The official bar guide to darts / by Patrick Chaplin.
      p. cm.
Includes bibliographical references and index.
ISBN 978-1-4027-5524-8
1. Darts (Game) I. Title.
GV1565.C43 2010
794.3--dc22

10 9 8 7 6 5 4 3 2 1

Published by Sterling Publishing Co., Inc.
387 Park Avenue South, New York, NY 10016
© 2010 by Patrick Chaplin
Distributed in Canada by Sterling Publishing
c/o Canadian Manda Group, 165 Dufferin Street,
Toronto, Ontario, Canada M6K 3H6
Distributed in the United Kingdom by GMC Distribution Services
Castle Place, 166 High Street, Lewes, East Sussex, England BN7 1XU
Distributed in Australia by Capricorn Link (Australia) Pty. Ltd.
P.O. Box 704, Windsor, NSW 2756, Australia

Sterling ISBN 978-1-4027-5524-8

For information about custom editions, special sales, premium and
corporate purchases, please contact Sterling Special Sales
Department at 800-805-5489 or specialsales@sterlingpublishing.com.

~ CONTENTS ~

Acknowledgments	v	**Chapter 3: The Basic Games**	30

Acknowledgments v

Introduction vii

Chapter 1: The Equipment 1

The Background: Darts 2

The Background: Dartboards 5

Darts Today: Your Choice 7

The Dartboard Today 9

Setting Up a Darts Area 11

Setting Up the Dartboard 12

Measuring the Throw Line
(or Oche) 14

Lighting 14

Care and Maintenance 15

**Chapter 2: How to Play Darts:
The Basics** 19

The Grip 19

The Stance 21

The Throw 26

Movement Along the
Throw Line 28

Chapter 3: The Basic Games 30

501 30

Cricket 40

Chapter 4: Other Darts Games 48

Games Derived from Other
Games or Sports 49

Other Alternative Games 60

Fun Adaptations 75

Chapter 5: Improving Your Game 80

The Mathematics of Darts 80

Practice, Practice, and
More Practice 82

Preparation 87

Proficiency 87

Nerves 89

Temperament 89

Rituals 90

Dedication 90

Personal Fitness and Health 91

The Formal Rules 92

Chapter 6: The Dangers, and How to Avoid Them 93

Darts Safety 93

Gamesmanship 96

The Crowd 97

Staying Cool 97

Dartitis 98

Chapter 7: The History of Darts 100

Darts: The Early Years 100

The Game Catches On 102

The First Boom 104

The Second Boom—
and Beyond 105

The History of Darts in the
United States 107

A Brief History of Electronic
("Soft-Tip") Darts 109

Chapter 8: Darts Etiquette, and Other Helpful Information 111

The Darts Referee 113

Where to Play 113

Chapter 9: Women's Darts 115

A Brief History of
Women's Darts 115

Women and Darts 117

Chapter 10: Tournaments 119

Some Key Tournaments
Past and Present 120

Legends of the Game 125

Chapter 11: Additional Equipment and Accessories 137

Flights 137

Shafts 138

Nonslip Finger Wax 139

Check-Out Tables 139

Darts Scorers 140

Darts Wallet and Cases 140

Darts: Adding Weight 141

Earplugs 141

Personalized Merchandise 142

Chapter 12: Gameshot! Final Advice and the Future 143

Appendix A: Singles, Doubles, and Triples Combination Chart 145

Appendix B: Outshot Chart 146

Appendix C: Darts Glossary 148

Appendix D: Further Reading and Other Resources 157

Appendix E: Tournament Rules 164

Appendix F: Abbreviations 176

Illustration Credits 176

Index 177

About the Author 182

ACKNOWLEDGMENTS

This book would never have seen the light of day without the love and support of others. I am fortunate to have a good number of friends who have helped me along the way.

My thanks to Vince Bluck, managing director of Nodor International, and to Ian Flack, sales and marketing director of the WINMAU Dartboard Company, for their support over recent years and their continued sponsorship of my ongoing research. I also appreciate the advice, information, and guidance received in the past from Robert Pringle at Harrows Darts Technology, Edward Lowy at Unicorn, and Tommy Cox of the Professional Darts Corporation. Thanks, too, to Olly Croft OBE, director of the British Darts Organisation (BDO), for advice on specific rules, to Buddy Bartoletta, president of the American Darts Organization, for permission to publish the ADO Tournament Rules in Appendix E, and author Chris Carey, particularly for expert guidance relating to cricket. I am also extremely grateful to Freddie and Pat Williams for their contributions relating to refereeing the sport of darts and dart averages.

In darts publishing, I record my appreciation of Tony Wood, former editor of *Darts World*, who gave me the first opportunity to write about darts in his magazine back in 1985, which is effectively where this book started. I also thank Jay Tomlinson from *Bull's-Eye News* for publishing my work from time to time. This helped to raise awareness of my research in the United States and Canada.

My thanks go to my webmaster David King (of www.Darts501.com) and Chris Barrell, who both provided a number of the images for this book. Others who provided images are acknowledged in the Illustration Credits on page 176. David King also provided the chart on page 146 and most welcome technical assistance.

For various other important reasons, I would like to thank my dad, Albert Chaplin; my wife, Maureen; Peter Gordon (at Puzzlewright Press); eight-time World Women's Darts Champion Trina Gulliver; my former "webmistress" Sheila Handley; Glen Huff, president of the Emerald City Darts Organization; Paul "Dartoid" Seigel; three-time World Professional Darts Champion John Lowe; and pub games expert Arthur R. Taylor— and, of course, the guys with whom I still share a dartboard once a week and whose company helps keep me sane, if not a little inebriated, namely, Colin Barrell and Bob Wilson.

Thanks also to Andrew Brisman for helping transform my 100,000 word manuscript into the book you are holding.

Finally, I would like to record my thanks to two great men of darts who are no longer with us. In the late 1980s, both John Ross, former president of the National Darts Association of Great Britain (NDAGB), and Noel E. Williamson, author of the book *Darts*, published in 1968, and one of England's first darts coaches, encouraged me to pursue my research into darts.

Although they never lived to see this book completed, I am sure in my heart that they would have approved.

~INTRODUCTION~

Today, darts is one of the most popular sports and recreational activities on the planet.

Darts can be played and enjoyed by anyone, regardless of class, sex, creed, education, color, height, weight, build, age, or ability. It is easy to learn and the equipment required to play will suit almost any budget. It is accessible and educational and, above all, can be an excellent social experience. Darts can be played for fun by young and old or it can be played seriously in leagues.

From its modest origins in the public houses of England, darts has taken less than one hundred years to become one of the most popular organized sports in the world. Darts can be found in pubs, clubs, rec centers, and schools around the world. Millions more choose to play for fun at home, either on a real bristle dartboard, perhaps hung on the garage wall or the door of a den, or on one of the safer alternatives for young children, such as magnetic darts or darts with Velcro®-like soft tips. The opportunities are endless.

Darts, originally linked primarily with pubs and alcohol, has now generally begun to shed that image and appeal to wider markets.

Such has been the progress of the sport in recent years that, at the time of this writing, even Iran boasts at least 500,000 darts players (both men and women). In the UK, darts is currently experiencing a renaissance. Its popularity waned following the heady days of the late 1970s and early 1980s, which created household names such as Eric "The Crafty

Cockney" Bristow, John "Old Stoneface" Lowe, and John Thomas "Jocky" Wilson. But the sport has gained new life as a result of the Professional Darts Corporation (PDC), particularly on satellite TV, and it is very much on the rise worldwide.

In America, too, darts became extremely popular in the early 1980s and created national stars, including Joe Baltadonis, Jerry Umberger, and Conrad Daniels. Although the rise of soft-tip (electronic) darts during the late 1980s seemed to signal the end of steel-tip darts in America, there are significant signs today that both forms can coexist.

Thus, the time is right for *The Official Bar Guide to Darts.*

The sole purpose of this book is to give *all* darts players—from raw beginners to those seeking to play at the highest level—everything they need to know. This is not simply another basic tuition book. It is a complete guide to the sport of darts, which covers everything from the history of the sport through the equipment required to how to play and how to improve your game.

There are even brief profiles of some of the top professional players in the world, both past and present.

Although this book concentrates on the British steel-tip version of the game, electronic darts is not ignored and, where necessary, essential differences between steel-tip and soft-tip darts are highlighted throughout the text.

For those who simply wish to learn how to play darts, chapter 1 (The Equipment) and chapter 2 (How to Play Darts: The Basics) will be a good start. Once you're comfortable with the standard games of 301, 501, and cricket, the book offers more than twenty alternative games that you can play on a standard dartboard. It also features a glossary of the colorful jargon peculiar to the sport.

Throughout the text, the term *darts player* is used, although I am aware that *shooter* is more popular in many parts of the United States. Similarly, when referring to the center of the dartboard, I use the more common term *bull's-eye*, rather than *double-bull* or *cork*, while the word *oche* is used in preference to the traditional spelling *hockey* to describe the point from which a player throws. More generally, within the text the words *throw line* are used. Importantly, wherever I refer to *he, his,* or *him* in the text, I mean this in a gender-neutral way to embrace *she, hers,* and *her.* Quotes from British sources have been Americanized and have had their spelling changed to American English—except for the word *Organisation* in an organization's name.

Though I have made every effort to define specific darts terms when they are introduced, you should be able to find any unfamiliar term in Appendix C. (This will be of particular use if you skip around the book.)

I have written this book in order to share my knowledge of and my enthusiasm for darts with you. I've played for local pubs and clubs (sometimes in a league but mostly on a casual basis) for more than four decades and I've researched the sport for over twenty years. Yes, I've won a few darts trophies in my time, but I am not a professional darts player. I cannot promise that *The Official Bar Guide to Darts* will turn you into a pro. But I can guarantee that it will enhance your own enjoyment of the sport.

If you are currently playing, I hope this book will encourage you to improve your game. If you are a novice, I trust that this book will enable you to take up darts, develop your game and style, and enjoy yourself. If you are simply interested in sports in general and wish to know more about darts, then this book is for you, too.

Good darting to you all.

Patrick Chaplin

Maldon, Essex, England

1

~THE EQUIPMENT~

Like everything in life, there's no point in going about any task without the right equipment. In darts, the two main pieces of equipment you must have are a good set of darts and a quality dartboard.

Some may think that the old dartboard that dad played on when he was a kid—the one that's been hanging inside the garage for years—and the set of mismatched darts with odd flights that your granddad found in a cupboard and gave to you, are ideal to start with and represent an investment-free introduction to the game. While such gestures are appreciated, this is not the best way to prepare you for what could become a long career of darts playing.

New equipment is essential if you want a firm foundation on which to learn to play darts. Put another way: To become a good "dartist," you must start with a blank canvas. Bad workers always blame their tools and, if you play with someone else's old darts and a decaying dartboard, you will play badly and you will blame dad and granddad. (There's more to darts equipment than merely your darts and the dartboard, but that's all this chapter will deal with for the moment. I deal with other darts-related accessories in chapter 11.)

Before examining the darts and dartboards of today, it is useful to look back at what equipment our predecessors played with and examine how darts and dartboards have developed over the years.

THE BACKGROUND: DARTS

There are many theories on how the dart evolved. Many believe that the first wooden darts were broken arrows, sharpened and then thrown at the ends of wine casks. Another school of thought argues that crossbow bolts were the precursors of modern darts, there being some evidence to show that firing crossbow bolts into the end of ale tuns (barrels) was an indoor English tavern pastime two hundred years ago. However, "puff and dart," a tavern game dating back to at least the sixteenth century, in which small darts were blown through a tube at a numbered target, is the half-great-grandparent of the modern dart.

All these theories involve a small dartlike object projected at a target, but the surprise is that the original darts used in the game we know today were not English at all, but French! *Sacre bleu!* The first darts used by the masses arrived in England in the mid- to late-nineteenth century, imported by fancy goods companies, along with other French woodworked items, including cabinets, tables, and other furniture. The importers' demand was initially drawn from fairgrounds that had introduced darts stalls into their list of new attractions.

Not surprisingly, those darts were known in Britain as "French darts." The body of the dart was made entirely of wood, with a metal point inserted at one end and three or four turkey feathers stuck on at the other end to serve as flights (see Figure 1). For many years, these darts were the most popular, since they were sold singly and were very cheap. However, this type of dart was very light and, at times, difficult to control. So varying weights were introduced, the extra weight (or "loading") being achieved by the addition of a ring of lead around the body of the dart or by drilling out the center of the dart from the point end, inserting a small amount of molten lead, and then replacing the point (see Figure 2). Such darts were often provided by the pub owner and were known as "house darts." This way, customers did not need to purchase their own darts.

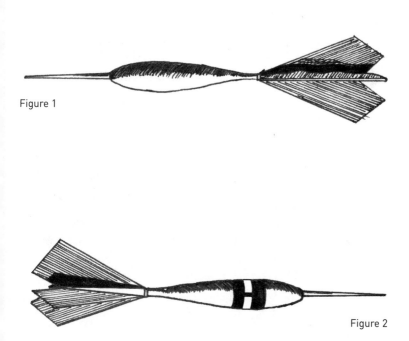

Figure 1

Figure 2

As darts became increasingly popular in England in the 1920s and 1930s, the darts themselves became more sophisticated and attracted more interest from UK-based suppliers. Light engineering companies turned their attention to darts and manufactured the first brass dart barrels (see Figure 3). With brass, darts players were no longer restricted to the French dart. Brass darts barrels were produced in all shapes, sizes, and weights, and quickly became the most popular form of dart in general play. Despite this, French darts remained popular with some old-timers for many years and, indeed, are still available today from specialized suppliers.

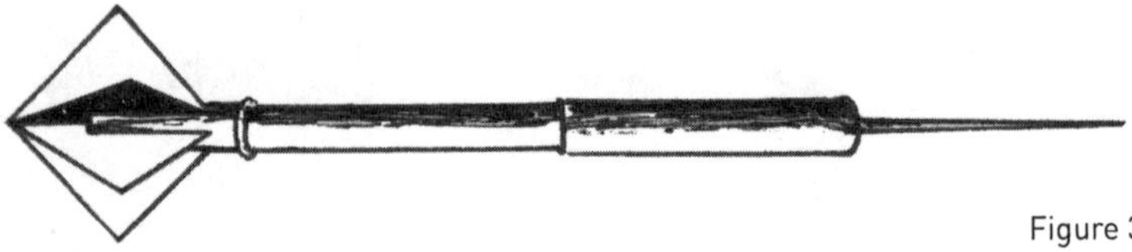

Figure 3

With the introduction of brass darts, it seemed as though the days of the feather flights were numbered. The brass darts were fitted with cane and slit crosswise at the far end. A folded paper or cardboard flight was inserted in the slit. Not everyone liked the lack of feathers, so the brass barrels were machined with threads that would take an adapter, into which feather flights were inserted (see Figure 4). Brass darts were to remain the most popular type of darts until the early 1970s, when tungsten alloy darts (commonly known as "tungstens") began to appear.

Figure 4

Introduced in response not only to the increasing popularity of darts in the 1970s but also because the players demanded more efficient "tools of the trade," tungsten darts were received with great enthusiasm. The benefit of tungsten in the manufacture of darts is that tungsten is denser than brass and thus what had previously been a bulky brass dart of, say, 25 grams, became a superslim tungsten dart of the exact same weight. (However, darts cannot simply be made out of tungsten. Pure tungsten is very brittle and difficult to machine, so the manufacturers create an alloy by combining tungsten powder with another element, usually copper or nickel.)

This breakthrough enabled players to leave more space when shooting at a target, for example triple 20. In contrast to thick brass darts, streamlined tungsten darts leave more room for the incoming darts and obscure a lot less of the target.

Throughout the late 1970s and early 1980s, the number of players using brass darts declined rapidly until it became a rare sight indeed to see anyone throwing brass darts either in bars or in major competitions. Today tungsten darts remain the choice of champions and new darts players alike. Brass darts have been more or less consigned to a supplementary role; they are the type of darts usually supplied in dartboard sets for young people and are still often "house darts."

THE BACKGROUND: DARTBOARDS

The dartboard is a descendent of the archery target (in miniature), made more complicated by the addition of segments and higher scoring rings. A small concentric archery target (see Figure 5) would not have proved

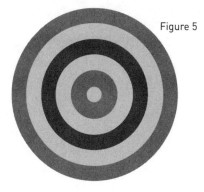

Figure 5

popular for very long indoors because experienced players would have enough skill to hit the bull's-eye (100 points) with comparative ease from close range. The dartboard was improved by the addition of individual wires (made by skilled wireworkers) to segregate the numbered segments. In later years, these wires would be manufactured as a one-piece unit.

By the late 1920s, a standardized dartboard was introduced (see Figure 6) and remains the most popular dartboard today throughout the world. However, the "standard" dartboard (also known as the "London" board) was not an overnight success in the UK. Initially, it had to compete with other target boards used in some localities. These have come to be known as "regional dartboards" and were usually named after their region of origin, such as the Yorkshire Doubles, the Kent Doubles, the London Fives, and the Manchester boards.

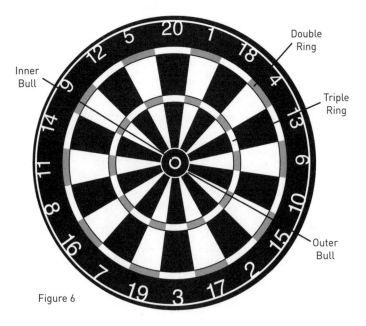

Figure 6

Traditionally, dartboards have been constructed of wood, usually elm or poplar. Both are soft woods and are thus easy to cut and shape and to receive the incoming darts. In the early 1930s, as the first darts boom took off in England, Nodor, a London-based company, filed a patent application for a new type of dartboard. Made of compressed sisal fiber, this dartboard became known as the "bristle" dartboard and had many advantages over the wooden dartboard. The wooden dartboards had to be soaked overnight in a metal container or even a sink or bath; otherwise they would dry out and crack. However well they were maintained, these boards had a limited life. By contrast, the bristle dartboard was long lasting, did not need soaking, and was more resistant to damage by darts than the elm or poplar board. In addition, with the bristle dartboard, when darts were removed from the board, the sisal fiber closed the hole behind it.

But the cost of bristle dartboards put them out of reach for ordinary people. Although these dartboards sold in sufficient numbers to enable Nodor to continue making them, bristle dartboards would not become the standard type of dartboard for most match play until the 1970s, when Dutch elm disease destroyed the supply of wood. Today, wooden dartboards are rare and bristle boards are seen almost everywhere steel-tip darts is played.

DARTS TODAY: YOUR CHOICE

Since the advent of brass barrels, darts have consisted of four pieces: the point, the barrel, the shaft, and the flight (see Figure 7). Nowadays, tungsten darts are the choice of most players, but if you are just starting out there are still a wide variety of less expensive brass darts available. Standard darts have a rigid, fixed point, yet today spring-loaded darts are available with a metal point constructed in such a way that it is free, so that when the point hits the dartboard, the rest of the dart effectively hammers the point into

Figure 7

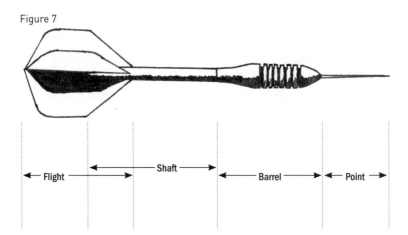

Flight ← → Shaft ← → Barrel ← → Point →

the dartboard. With so many different styles of darts, shafts, and flights, the permutations are endless and the choices bewildering.

So how can you determine which dart is best for you? Many players decide by simple trial and error. Your local darts supply shop may have a few types to try out. You can also locate many darts retailers online, though it's always best to test the darts if possible. You might be able to borrow darts from experienced friends and see which you find to your liking. Try different weights. In the early days, darts were sold only in three weights—light, medium, or heavy—but today darts are available in many weights and lengths, although for official tournament play the maximum weight allowable for steel-tip darts is 50 grams (18 grams for soft-tip) and the maximum length 12 inches (30.5 cm). Experiment. It is doubtful that the first set of darts you purchase will be your last.

It is generally recommended that first-time players start with a medium-weight dart, say, 21–23 grams, with a medium-length shaft and standard-shaped flights. If during testing the dart falls below your intended target area, then the dart is too heavy for you. If the dart lands above the intended target or flies off in a totally different direction than the one you anticipated, then the dart is too light. Change to either a heavier or a lighter dart and aim for the same target again—and note the improvement. In addition, keeping the same dart barrel but changing either the length of the shaft or the shape of the flight (or both) might improve the way you and your darts perform.

An expensive set of darts will not turn you into a star player or even a good bar player. The bottom line is this: Choose a set you're comfortable with.

Those playing soft-tip darts will have a more restricted choice. As the name suggests, in electronic darts the darts have softer tips, usually of tough plastic, since a metal point penetrating the electronic dartboard would certainly cause major problems. Due to the sensitivity of the electronic dartboard, the weight of darts does not tend to exceed 18 grams. However, manufacturers are now making heavier soft-tip darts up to 24–25 grams in weight.

THE DARTBOARD TODAY

In steel-tip darts, the standard bristle dartboard is by far the most familiar and common target in both competitive and casual darts today.

The standard dartboard is 18 inches (45.5 cm) in diameter with a scoring area that has a diameter of 13¼ inches (33.7 cm). (The normal dimensions of a standard board are shown in Figure 8.) By looking at the dartboard (see Figure 6), you will note that the scoring area is divided into twenty main segments numbered 1 to 20, but not sequentially. The numbers are distributed in such a way to ensure that accuracy is rewarded and inaccuracy penalized. For example, note the position of the 20. On the left-hand side of that major number is the 5 and, to the right, the smallest number, 1. Thus, failure to hit the larger number will result in a much-reduced score. The segments are divided by metal wires (commonly

Figure 8

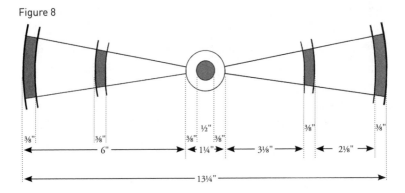

known as the "spider") so that the numbers are properly delineated and there can be no argument about which segment a dart has hit.

Around the circumference of the scoring area is another ring, a series of segments ⅜ inch (10 mm) wide. This is the double ring and any dart landing in that area scores double the number. Inside the target area, midway between the double ring and the center of the dartboard, is another ring, another series of segments: the triple ring. Darts landing in that area score three times the number of the segment.

In the center of the dartboard is the bull's-eye. Before the introduction of the standard dartboard, this was, as in archery, the highest possible scoring target. In darts the bull's-eye has a value of 50 points and also counts as double 25. In addition to the bull's-eye, the standard dartboard also includes an "outer bull" worth 25 points. With the introduction of the triple ring, the highest score moved from the center of the dartboard to over three inches (7.6 cm) above the bull's-eye: triple 20, scoring 60 points. Darts is therefore the only target game where hitting a particular mark off-center scores more points than striking the actual bull's-eye!

Each scoring area of a standard dartboard is colored. If you look directly at a dartboard properly positioned on the wall in front of you,

you'll notice that the double 20 is red and that, going clockwise, the double 1 is green and that the red-green sequence is continued around the dartboard. Similarly, the triple 20 is red, the triple 1 is green, and so on around the board. The large and small single scoring areas of the 20 segment are black and those equivalent areas of the 1 are white and so it alternates around the dartboard. The outer bull (or "outer cork" or "25") is always green and the bull's-eye (or "cork" or "50") is red. The non-scoring area around the edge of the dartboard is always black.

In the past, black and yellow segments were common and, in the case of some wooden dartboards, there was no color at all, except that of the natural wood. Brighter colors are often used in the design of children's dartboards. However, the red, green, white, and black colors of the modern dartboard are regarded today as "standard" in all league matches and professional competitions and tournaments.

The non-scoring area has two functions. First, it provides a safe area for errant darts to land when a player misses his or her intended target, commonly known in the UK as being "off the island," and, second, it provides space for the wire ring containing the numbers of each segment to be placed.

Familiarize yourself with the structure and segmentation of the dartboard.

SETTING UP A DARTS AREA

When playing darts in a bar, a club, or a rec center, the dartboard and throwing area should already be set up in accordance with the standard rules of darts play. At home it will be up to you to be certain that your "oche" (throw line) conforms to current rules of darts. Otherwise you will not be helping yourself if, say, the length of the throw is shorter than standard.

Please make sure that, if you are setting up your darts area in an apartment, the wall on which the dartboard is to hang is *not* a shared wall. Whatever you may think about your own enthusiasm for darts, your next-door neighbors are unlikely to appreciate the "thud-thud-thud" of dart after dart, day after day, and night after night. Also, try not to hang the dartboard on the back of a door. Someone may open it while you are throwing! Also ensure that the dartboard is not hung above a heater or radiator.

If you are planning to set up your own area at home, at the office, or in the garage, use the specifications that follow in the next section. (You might want to avoid the garage because exposure to the elements will not be kind to your dartboard.)

To begin with, find an area approximately 12 feet long by 5 or 6 feet wide (3.6 m x 1.5–1.8 m). This will be sufficient room for your "darts court" and give you enough space to comfortably move around.

SETTING UP THE DARTBOARD

Hang the dartboard on the wall in a vertical position with the center of the bull's-eye exactly 5 feet 8 inches (173 cm) from the floor. The 20 segment must be at the top and, vertically below it, the 3 segment. The board must be firmly affixed to the wall to ensure no movement either during play or when darts are removed.

Most of today's quality dartboards come with a dartboard mounting kit, which consists of a bracket (to affix to the wall), bracket mounting screws, a board mounting screw, three "feet" (to prevent the dartboard from coming into contact with the wall), and an installation and instructional booklet. Some of this essential equipment and the instructions may be missing if you buy a secondhand dartboard, so it is best to purchase one new.

An alternative to affixing the dartboard to the wall is to install a wooden cabinet to house the dartboard. If the dartboard is not housed in a cabinet, errant darts will make numerous small holes in walls and the points of the darts will invariably be damaged if they strike hard walls (as in a garage) instead of the dartboard. Darts cabinets most commonly include doors that can be closed to ward off sunlight, which can dry out and discolor a board. Both cabinet doors usually have scoreboards on them and top-quality cabinets might also include places in which to store your darts.

If you do not purchase a cabinet, then you will need to install a scoreboard that can be seen from the throw line. This can take the form of a simple blackboard or dry-erase board on which the scores can be marked. Those with more money can purchase an electronic scoreboard. (See chapter 11 for more details on the types of scoreboards and other darts accessories that are available.)

Often the type of flooring is the last thing to be considered, but this is of the utmost importance. In a house, wooden floors must be protected. If not, then it will not be long before they appear to have been invaded by woodworm. Bouncing or badly thrown darts will land with the point in the floor the vast majority of the time. A carpet might appear to protect the floor but usually all it does is hide the damage beneath.

Consider a dart mat made from heavy-duty nonslip rubber with an integral white line that indicates the standard throwing distance of 7 feet 9¼ inches (2.37 m) and the soft-tip distance of 8 feet (2.45 m). The mat can be rolled up and stored away when not in use. However, if placed over a carpet, the mats tend to move when walked on, so take care to ensure that the throw line is properly measured and maintained at all times. (See the next section, "Measuring the Throw Line [or Oche].")

Try to position the dartboard so that your play is not impeded by anything. For example, if the dartboard is positioned too close to a wall that runs parallel to the throw, you may literally run into a wall as you try for a better angle on a target. Watch out, too, for bright sunlight that will affect your view of your intended target. Also make sure that valuable furniture, televisions, computers, and ornaments are not close to the area, as these can be damaged by rebounding or badly thrown darts.

MEASURING THE THROW LINE (OR OCHE)

Once the dartboard is fitted on the wall in the best position, the distance of the throw line (or "oche," sometimes also called the "toe-line") can be established. The standard distance from which to throw a dart is 7 feet 9¼ inches (2.37 m), and it is vitally important that this is accurately measured.

To achieve this, a plumb line should be dropped from the bull's-eye; that is, from the face of the board to the floor. The line is *not* measured from the wall but from the point at which the plumb line meets the floor. Then measure horizontally along the floor at a right angle to the wall a 7 foot 9¼ inch line. Mark where that measurement terminates. This can be done with masking or gaffer tape or, preferably, with a piece of metal or wood affixed permanently to the floor. If using wood or metal, ensure that it is parallel with the dartboard and that, when the leading foot is placed against it, the player is actually toeing the line at exactly 7 feet 9¼ inches. In competition the length of the metal or wooden throw-line is measured at a minimum of 24 inches (0.61 m). Marking the line on the floor in chalk is not recommended, as such a line is prone to be rubbed out with constant play. When the line is redrawn, it can begin to creep forward or back.

No player can step over or on this line until after the throw has been completed. Players can move along the throw line as far as they wish but only in an imaginary straight line extended from the throw line.

Your completed darts court should look like the one shown in Figure 9.

LIGHTING

Efficient lighting must be provided if you are going to take darts seriously. Without a clear view of the dartboard, or with part of it in shade, you will never play your best.

Players should not depend on the light coming from a bulb in the center of the room or garage. A separate strong light should be set up in

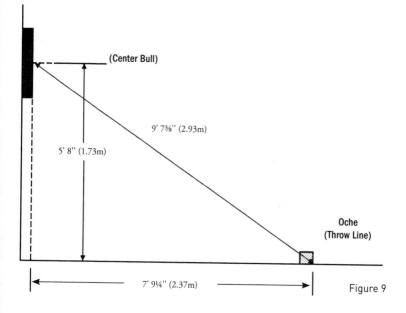

(Center Bull)

9' 7⅜" (2.93m)

5' 8" (1.73m)

Oche
(Throw Line)

7' 9¼" (2.37m)

Figure 9

the ceiling in front of and above the dartboard to concentrate the light solely in that area. It must be high enough not to be struck by incoming darts. If the light is not adequately shielded, it might shine in a players' eyes—hardly conducive to good play.

With modern technology has come innovation in dartboard illumination. One of the most recent is the Circumluminator, manufactured by Nuvolux of Austin, Texas. This is a lighting system that embraces the dartboard by surrounding it with light and banishing shadows.

CARE AND MAINTENANCE

The equipment used by darts players must be well-maintained. If the tools of your trade are not in the best order, how can you expect to do a good job? It would be like a Formula One driver going to the starting line with a wheel missing or a football player leaving his helmet in the locker room.

Darts

To protect your darts from accidental damage, always carry them in a plastic pouch or protective case and store them safely there between matches. If you are unsure about the venue and fear possible theft, keep the darts in your possession when they are not in use. If you are worried about losing your darts, buy a second set, that is exactly the same, just to be on the safe side.

Points and Barrels

The metal points of your darts should remain sharp at all times. With damaged points, you risk more "bounce-outs," where a dart hits a wire and bounces off the dartboard. Check the points every time before you play.

Dart sharpeners can be purchased for a small sum from darts suppliers. Usually this piece of equipment is a hollowed-out, cylinder-shaped piece of abrasive material. The sharpener is held in one hand, the dart inserted and rotated inside the cylinder with the other hand, until a fine point is obtained. All points will gradually wear down with use; this can affect the balance of your dart and therefore your throw. So check them regularly and have them replaced when necessary. Clearly a bar or casual player would not need to have their points replaced as regularly as a full-time professional player.

At first glance, dart barrels would not, perhaps, appear to need much attention. However, they should be checked regularly for burrs and nicks. Incoming darts may damage a barrel. Most darts players do not clean their darts barrels because polished barrels make the darts more difficult to handle. Those who do clean their barrels generally remove chalk or grease by using only tepid water and a drop of two of liquid soap.

Shafts

Darts shafts (or "stems," as they are also called), the small pieces of plastic or metal that screw into the barrels and into which the flights are secured, need to be checked before and after every game. They are very susceptible to damage. Metal shafts can become burred and distorted. Plastic shafts break easily. Both can become chipped or warped with use. Shafts can also become loose and that will affect the whole flight of the dart. Watch professional darts players and see how often they instinctively check both their shafts and their flights between throws.

Flights

Flights are the "feathers" on a dart that make it more stable and aerodynamic. They receive the most damage during play, since they are often hit by other darts. Flights can also be damaged if a player pulls all his darts out of the dartboard at the same time with one hand—so don't do that. Most common flights today are made of thermo-sealed laminated polyester and come in a variety of shapes and designs. (For examples of flight shapes, see chapter 11.)

Despite the durability of such flights, they should be checked regularly. Make sure that each one of the four fins of the flight is at a ninety-degree angle to the adjacent one. If you find them to be damaged or misshapen, replace them immediately. Always check that each flight, whether made of plastic, paper, or cardboard, is firmly attached to the shaft and, as with the shafts, check them before each throw. Fortunately, most flights are reasonably priced and players can afford to carry at least one spare set with them at all times. Top players often discard and replace their flights after each match. If you can afford to do that, then do it.

Dartboards

Modern bristle dartboards do not maintain themselves and do not last forever. There are a number of steps you can take to ensure a longer life for your dartboard.

Like any other material, the sisal fibers in a bristle dartboard will dry out, especially after constant exposure to sunlight. Once the dartboard has become hard and the sisal fibers less flexible, darts will begin to fall out. Keep your dartboard housed in a cabinet and keep the doors of the cabinet firmly closed when the dartboard is not in use.

Most darts players concentrate on the "red bit," the triple 20, as that is the highest scoring segment on the board. That area will become worn, the sisal will loosen, and darts will fall out. Also, the wires surrounding the triple 20 bed will become pockmarked and bend out of shape. To ensure even wear of the dartboard, remove the number ring from the board and then rotate the dartboard in a clockwise direction two segments until the "red bit" of triple 12 is in the triple 20 position. Replace the number ring, check that the dartboard is straight, and commence play again. If you rotate the dartboard this way once every month, you'll guarantee even use of the "red bits." (You may need to rotate it more frequently depending on how often you play.)

If you have a dartboard that does not have a movable numbers ring or one where the numbers and segments are merely printed on the face of the board, no routine maintenance is possible.

Now that you have acquired your darts and dartboard, set up your throwing area, and learned how to care for your "tools," let's learn to play darts.

2

~HOW TO PLAY DARTS~

THE BASICS

With the equipment bought, the dartboard hung (or you have found a place to play), and your enthusiasm growing, it is time to learn the fundamentals of playing darts. This chapter deals with how to grip a dart, how to stand properly at the throw line ("the stance"), and how to throw, or, rather, release the dart correctly. It also clarifies when it is wise to move along the throw line and introduces you to two of the most common darts games—501 and cricket.

To play darts well, you need to grasp the fundamentals. After learning the fundamentals of the sport, you will bring your own personal influence to bear, customizing the way you play.

THE GRIP

Gripping a dart is akin to holding a pen or pencil. Lay a dart and a pencil side by side on a table and pick each one up in turn with your natural throwing hand. You will see that you use the same, comfortable grip for both. The dart is held between the thumb, the index finger, and the second finger, as shown in Figure 10. This is known as the "standard grip" and is the usual starting point for all darts players.

What is not clear from the drawing is that the thumb naturally sits under the center of gravity. If you are uncertain as to where exactly the center of gravity is on a dart, then you can determine it by placing the dart across the top of one extended finger and moving the dart from one

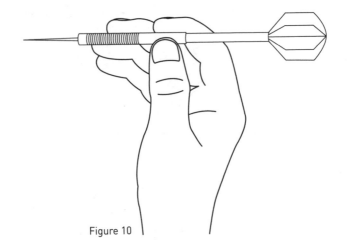

Figure 10

side to the other, as necessary, until it balances on the finger. Note where the point of balance is—that is the center of gravity. By using the center of gravity, the weight of the dart is evenly distributed and you will be "flighting" each dart properly. Theoretically, you will have more control over where it eventually lands.

The index finger is placed on top of the barrel and the second finger extended practically to the end of the barrel. Both fingers and thumb should apply pressure to the barrel to establish a firm grip—yet a grip as light as possible—without causing the dart to drop out of your hand. Practice this grip. Simply hold the dart in your hand and become used to this simple act. Get comfortable with it. Put the dart down and then pick it up again. The grip will soon become second nature.

In reality, no two darts players grip their darts in exactly the same way. Factors such as the size of the player's hands, the preferred style of darts barrel, the length of the shafts, or the design of particular flights might dictate a modification of the standard grip. Take, for example, the grip adopted by five-time World Professional Darts Champion Eric Bristow: His middle finger actually touches the point of the dart and his little finger is cocked and pointing skyward. Nonetheless, Bristow's grip evolved from the standard grip.

Each player's ultimate grip will develop through trial and error. By taking action to compensate for poor accuracy; by moving the thumb and/or fingers up and down the barrel; and by experimenting with different flights, shafts, and dart weights, players zero in on a comfortable and satisfactory grip—one that guarantees the smooth and accurate release of each dart at all times.

If you have problems gripping the dart, perhaps the darts barrel is too smooth. Try switching to a set of darts with knurled barrels. Alternatively, carry a stick of chalk or a small resin block (known as finger grip wax) with you to rub on the barrels to enhance your grip.

Finally, check your own hands. Make certain they are warm and clean before a game. Cold, stiff fingers will not enhance your play. Greasy fingers can cause your grip to slip. Check your fingernails, too. Rough nails can catch on the barrel and sometimes result in a wayward dart.

THE STANCE

Before going on to throw darts, it is important to know how to stand correctly at the throw line, which will ensure the best and most accurate flight of your darts.

When you first stand behind the throw line and face the dartboard, take your three darts and throw each one as best you can toward the center of the dartboard. How successful were you? Did your body (apart from your throwing arm) move at all? *Nothing* is supposed to move except your throwing arm. Any movement of any other part of the body while throwing—such as one leg swinging about, the raising of a heel, the involuntary sticking out of the tongue, or deliberately leaning forward or sideways—will result in inaccuracy.

If such extraneous movement characterizes your game, you are unlikely to become an accomplished darts player. If that is not your aim, then simply adopt a stance that feels comfortable for you and enjoy your darts. However, while there are all kinds of different styles, one stance has emerged over the years as the most favored among experienced darts players.

To adopt this stance, first imagine a line that runs from a point where a plumb line from the center of the dartboard hits the floor and then runs along the floor in a straight line to the throw line. Note the point at which it meets the throw line and place your right foot against it, with your big toe pointing directly along that imaginary line to the dartboard. Then place your left foot slightly behind your right foot at an outward angle (see Figure 11). (Obviously, if you are left-handed, reverse this procedure.) In this position, rotate your trunk slightly so that when you raise your right arm to throw, not only is your right elbow pointing at the dartboard but it is also directly over your right toe. You will notice that slightly more weight falls on your right leg and foot. For good reason, this stance is known as "Best Foot Forward."

Another stance that has proved popular and has been successfully adopted by many players is the "side-footed stance," where the right foot

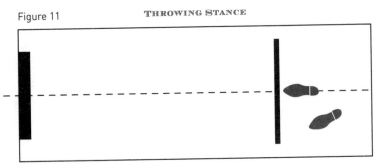

Figure 11   **THROWING STANCE**

Dartboard   Oche/Throwing Line

is placed parallel with the throw line and the left foot placed behind the right foot at an angle of approximately forty-five degrees (see Figure 12). This stance actually brings the thrower approximately six inches (15 cm) nearer to the target. Other stances include the one adopted by the late great English darts player Tom Barrett, who stood with his feet together, both pointing straight at the dartboard (see Figure 13). Five-time World Professional Darts Champion Eric "The Crafty Cockney" Bristow stood with his right foot turned with the instep edge fully against the throw line.

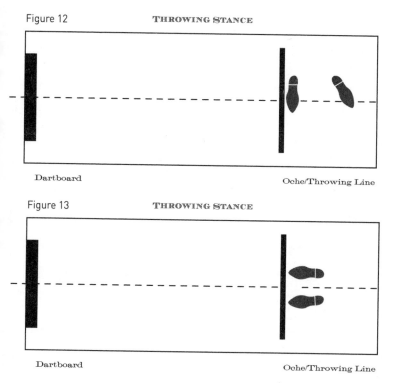

Figure 12   **THROWING STANCE**

Dartboard   Oche/Throwing Line

Figure 13   **THROWING STANCE**

Dartboard   Oche/Throwing Line

An awkward stance that is *not* recommended, yet appeals to some beginners, has the darter standing with his left foot forward and throwing with his right hand (or vice versa). Unless a player has contortionist skills, he will soon find that this stance poses difficulties. It forces him to twist his body and puts far too much movement into the throw.

As with the grip, darts players will eventually customize their stances to suit their own style. If neither of the two most popular stances detailed above is comfortable for you, then adopt a variation that feels right. If you are practicing and you rack up a decent score with three darts, stop before you walk forward to retrieve your darts, look down and make a mental note of where you are standing. Then stand in exactly the same position when you throw your next three darts.

Bottom line: If your stance is balanced and comfortable, with no superfluous movement, your darts will likely fly true.

WHAT TO WEAR

Before you actually throw that first dart, it is worth stopping a moment to consider what to wear when playing darts. As would be expected, comfort is the key.

In many old photographs of darts players in 1920s and 1930s England, the oche was awash with men in jackets, ties, and caps, but, of course, time moves on.

For men and women, casual, open-neck, short-sleeved shirts are now the norm. These are much less restrictive than long-sleeved shirts and allow freedom of movement of the arm and wrist, which is vital at all levels of darts play. Some players prefer their shirts with a top pocket in which to keep their darts safe and secure when not in play.

Pants are preferred by both sexes on the oche and, like the shirts, must be practical and comfortable and not be too tight or restrict movement. Of course, jeans can be worn in bar matches, but are usually banned in serious tournaments. The standard dress code for most tournaments is black pants and shoes. Also make sure that you keep pockets clear of any bulky items. Fat wallets, cigarettes, or bunches of keys may cause tightness and affect both your stance and throw. Hand them to a trusted friend while you play.

When deciding on footwear, think primarily about what shoe style is comfortable for you. This will ensure stability and balance at the throw line. Do not forget that socks should be comfortable too, and not restrict the movement of the feet too much.

It is not advisable to wear jewelry while playing darts, at least not the kind that might affect either your throw or your general movement. Some professional darts players seem awash in gold bangles and rings, but you will notice that such "bling" is rarely worn on the throwing hand. Except for perhaps a wedding band, the throwing hand should be clear of all obstructions at all times. On the other hand (literally) you might find jewelry containing gold equivalent to the holdings of Fort Knox, but that is not interfering with play. Wear only light necklaces or chains around the neck, as these can become restrictive and uncomfortable as a match proceeds. If you tend to wear a watch or bracelet on the wrist of your throwing arm, then it is advisable to remove it both in practice and when playing. Any undue movement of the watch or bracelet during play will affect your throw.

The choice of how you dress for a darts match in a local bar or club is ultimately yours, but remember that you are not standing at the oche to make a fashion statement. You are there to win the game. Dress sensibly, decently, comfortably, and look good. This can enhance your confidence and perhaps give you a psychological advantage over a less snappily dressed opponent. Remember, too, that in the more serious league and tournament competitions the dress code will be stipulated in the relevant organization's rules.

THE THROW

Having learned the grip and the stance, the next step is to master the actual throw. Although this may seem like a relatively simple task, the throw is the key element of your game and, therefore, demands more attention, effort, and practice than any other. You need to perfect a smooth, fluent, single action of the right (or left) arm to propel the dart precisely to its intended target.

Before approaching the throw line, prepare yourself mentally for the task. Shut out any external concerns you may have: File them away in the back of your mind until after the match, and apply yourself wholly to the game. If the room or venue is noisy, block the noise out and concentrate on the target. Coming to the line relaxed and confident is half the battle.

Check your stance and grip. Take hold of your first dart and slowly bring your arm up so that the dart is in a sighting position level with the right (or left) eye, almost but not actually touching your cheek. The closer you are to the cheek (without touching) the better, as this will increase the accuracy of the alignment of your eye with the intended target. Never lose sight of your dart by pulling it too far back. You must make sure that you can see the dart out of the corner of your eye while also focusing on the target in front of you. The throw is all about hand-eye coordination.

It is also very much about the position and control of the right (or left) arm. As you bring the dart up, make certain that your elbow is pointing at the dartboard and that it stays there throughout the throwing action. Consider the elbow as a pivot and bring the forearm back toward your face, ensuring throughout that the upper arm remains horizontal. Using the wrist as a second pivot, allow the hand to bring the dart a little further back toward the right (or left) ear but without ever losing sight of the dart.

With both the target and dart in sight, take careful aim. The elbow must still be pointing at the dartboard. With no movement of any other part of the body, move the forearm forward and, at the top of the arc prescribed by that action (that is just before your arm begins its downward path), release the dart with a light, smooth, fluid motion so it flies toward the target along the sight line (see Figure 14). At no time during the throw should you be looking anywhere other than at the intended target. If you release the dart too early, before it reaches the top of the arc, the dart will not hit the intended target but rather strike an area above it. Similarly, if you release the dart after the top of the arc, then the dart will land below the target.

Figure 14

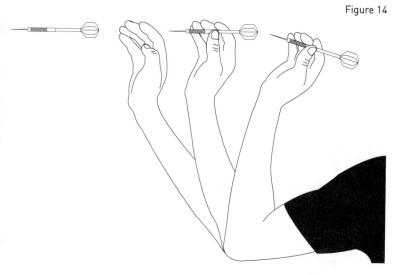

Many darts players do not keep their elbow tucked in. As the dart is released, the elbow jerks to the right—rather like the wing of an irritated chicken—and this superfluous action is bound to affect the direction of the dart. The only movement should come from the forearm and wrist.

Follow through with each throw. It is a situation similar to golf, where the golfer continues the motion of the club after the ball has been struck. The same is true of darts. Release the dart smoothly and complete the follow-through. Failure to do this will certainly affect the accuracy of your darts.

Most throwing styles generally follow the pattern described above. However, a number of players hold their darts in the right hand but line them up with the left eye, throwing in an arc from the left-hand side. Such players are known as "mixed laterals."

As for the speed of each throw, this varies from player to player. Some can be incredibly slow, taking their time over aiming and throwing each dart, while others complete their turn of three darts within seconds. Somewhere between the two is your optimum speed. To ensure the consistency and quality of your throw, find a speed and rhythm that suits you and your style of play. Each time you step up to the oche, throw each dart at the same speed with the same smooth, confident action.

Before moving on to the next section, there is one more issue that needs to be addressed—the errant third dart. Put simply, a great number of players find that, although the first and second darts go exactly where they should, the third (due perhaps to lack of concentration) tends to fall a little short of the proposed target. Indeed, Keith Deller, the 1983 Embassy World Professional Darts Champion, recognized that this was a problem. However, his solution was simple: "Throw the third dart just that little bit harder than the second dart." This is what Keith recommends and it might well work for you if you suffer from this common problem. However, if it doesn't work for you, you'll need to take a more critical look at your throw and your stance to address the glitch. Indeed, in some cases players have successfully overcome the "third dart syndrome" by practicing with *four* darts.

MOVEMENT ALONG THE THROW LINE

For many years, established darts players believed that, having adopted the stance, a player should *never* move along the throw line; that is, each of the three darts should be released from exactly the same position. A certain amount of wisdom underlies this advice. Throwing all three darts from a set position ensures conformity of throw.

However, there are certain times when this rule needs to be broken. Standing in exactly the same spot can work to your disadvantage (and to your opponent's advantage) if your target is obscured by an earlier dart. Staying where you are and trying to solve the problem by lobbing the next dart over the top of the earlier one is tantamount to "hoping for the best." It also increases the possibility of a following dart striking one already in the dartboard and bouncing out or being deflected into another segment and thus, clearly, makes no sense.

Fortunately, since the darts boom of the late 1970s, it has become common practice for players to move freely along the throw line in either direction. Moving slightly to the left or right of your established position often reveals more of the target. From a new angle, the dart that was obscuring the intended target can be a surprising help—the incoming dart may deflect off the barrel of the established dart into the required segment. Of course, remember to always settle yourself down and be comfortable with the new position.

Occasionally, movement along the throw line does not help. The target remains obscured. If the target is a finishing double (that is, the double required to win the game or match), then you have little choice but to throw and hope—unless there is another finishing combination. Clearly, if you are on double 1, then you have no choice but to go for it. But if you were throwing for score on triple 20, then the next option would be to play what is known as a "cover shot" where you change your target for the next highest triple, triple 19.

In general, the best advice is this: Only move along the throw line if it is absolutely necessary.

THE BASIC GAMES

501

The game of 501 is the most common game played in both serious and casual darts competitions throughout the world. (It is sometimes reduced to 301 in individual league play and increased to 701, 801, or even 1,001 in team play.) The idea of 501, or indeed any of the "01" games, is for one player or team of players to reduce their score to zero, finishing on a double, before their opponents.

ORIGINS OF "01" GAMES

In the very first games of darts, players would throw three darts and the one with the highest score with those three darts won the game. However, as the game increased in popularity and, through experience and practice, the target became easier to hit, darts became a little more sophisticated.

The original "01" in English public houses—301—was scored on a cribbage board. Cribbage is an old English pub card game—and older than darts—where scores derived from the value of cards are recorded by pegging holes on a wooden cribbage board.

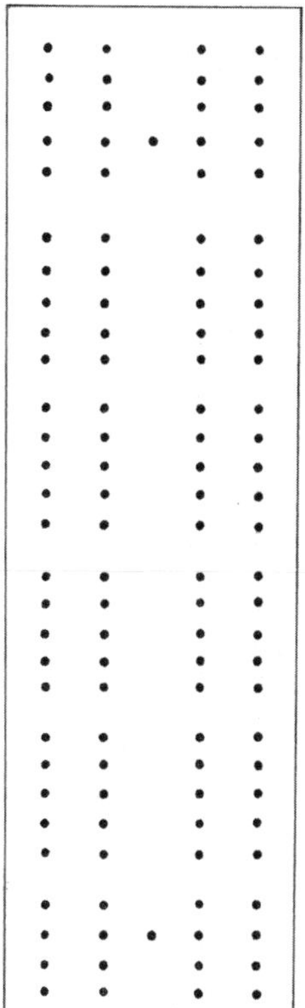

Each side of the cribbage board has two rows of thirty holes and one extra hole at each end. Scores are recorded on each side by use of two pegs (see Figure 15). To win the game, players have to achieve a given number of circuits of the board (60 holes) plus the one extra hole representing "home," making 61. Any game played on the cribbage board has to be a multiple of 60—plus 1. For example "twice round" would be 120 (plus 1) and "three times round" would be 180 (plus 1).

In the early days of modern darts, the score was recorded on the cribbage board and defined as "five times round" the board for a total of 300 (60 holes x 5) plus 1. Thus: 301. Using this method, players could see their score at every stage of play by looking at the cribbage board. Later, with the introduction of proper scoreboards, usually a type of blackboard and chalk, the cribbage boards were handed back to the card players.

Figure 15

Whether by coincidence or design, the "01" game helped prevent darts from becoming terribly boring. With the "01" game, it meant that players had to move away from the 20 segment—at least for a short while—in order to win the game. The double finish, required in all standard games of 501, also calls for more than just scoring skill.

Before a game of 501 begins, that number is written at the top of the scoreboard and each player's name or initials or team name is written beneath it on the left-hand side and the right-hand side:

501

MIKE	BILL

The order of play is usually determined by "bulling-up." Each player shoots for the bull's-eye and whoever's dart is nearest the center throws first. (In Professional Darts Corporation tournaments the "bulling-up" is different. The PDC requires the player(s) to hit the outer or inner bull; otherwise, a dart is considered "out of the bull.") Other methods include tossing a coin to decide, throwing for the bull's-eye with your "wrong hand" (the one you do not normally use to throw a dart), or simultaneously throwing all three darts at the board (known as "splashing"). In the latter case, the player with the highest total goes first in the game. When playing at a new venue, always check which rule applies.

There is a distinct advantage in throwing first because if players are evenly matched, the player who throws second is always playing catch-up. Some people equate this to tennis, in that the player throwing second has to "break the serve" of the player who began the game or, as it is more commonly called, the player needs to "take the darts" off his opponent.

On rare occasions, a confident player who wins the bull-up will allow his opponent to throw first. This is usually done as a psychological ploy.

Once it has been decided who throws first, the game can begin. In most games of 501, the player goes "straight in," meaning he begins scoring with his first dart. Each player throws three darts per turn and the winner is the first player who finishes the game by reducing his score to zero. The final dart must hit a double that reduces the score exactly to zero.

Sometimes, however, 501 is played with a "double in, double out" rule. In that case, in order to begin the game, a player must score a double—any double. As soon as he hits a double, his game officially begins and the value of that double—and that of any remaining darts on that turn—counts for score. No darts that strike the scoring area of the dartboard before the first double count.

Darts players want to finish a game of 501 in the fewest darts. For this reason, most players concentrate on the highest scoring segment—the "red bit" (triple 20). Three darts in this segment scores 180, the highest possible score in three darts on a standard dartboard.

However, the high scores will not necessarily win you the game. As Bobby George, a top English professional darts player, says, "Scoring's for show; doubles for dough." In other words, there's no point in being able to hit triple 20 repeatedly if you cannot hit the required double. No double, no win, no dough. You should practice hitting all segments of the dartboard with equal intensity. Also, think of your finish long before you reach that final double.

After each player has thrown his darts, his score is registered on the left under his name and his remaining score is indicated to the right. Thus a completed game of 501 (in which Mike has thrown first) might look as shown on page 34.

In this example, played "straight in," Mike is by far the more consistent player. Throughout the game he played very well and, after

501

MIKE		BILL	
100	401	60	441
80	321	25	416
80	241	20	396
100	141	45	351
81	60	180	171
Gameshot			

only twelve darts, was on an outshot of 141. Bill, on the other hand, had major problems with his scoring. Although he did rally a little toward the end of the match, with a maximum 180, it was too late by then. Mike shot out on 60, most likely going single 20, "double top" (double 20). Even if Mike had missed his outshot on 60, he would still have at least three more darts to win the game, as Bill had left himself a remaining score of 171, one of those "bogey numbers" where the game cannot be finished in three darts.

After a game is over, who throws first in the next game? In friendly competition, it's usually "Mugs away!"—that is, loser throws first. However, in more formally organized matches, players take turns going first, no matter who wins the previous game.

The "Bust" Rule

Before moving on to discuss outshots and the perfect game of 501, a word about the "bust" rule.

It is now accepted practice in the majority of darts leagues and competitions that if a player scores more than he needs (thereby busting or "bursting" his score), he reverts back to the score he had before any of his three darts were thrown. For example, a player requires 36 (double 18) for game. He shoots triple 18 (54 points) and therefore busts. His turn ends and his score returns to 36.

Confusion arose in the early days of darts when some forms of the rules allowed players to revert to the score achieved by the last *scoring* dart. For example, a player requires 37 points to finish the game. The player throws a single 5, leaving 32 (double 16). His second dart misses the double 16 and instead lands in double 8, leaving 16. The player requires another double 8 for game. Unfortunately, his third dart hits double 11 (22 points) and "busts" the score. Under the "last scoring dart" rule, the player does not revert to the 37 points he had at the beginning of his turn, but to 16 points, because his first and second darts counted for score.

As always, when you are unsure, you must check the local rules. Nowadays, the "bust" rule, where any bust returns you to your previous turn's score, will apply in 99 percent of the cases, but make sure that other 1 percent doesn't catch you unawares.

Finally, for absolute clarification, we can refer to the American Darts Organization's Rule 47, which states that the "Bust Rule will apply. If the player scores one less, equal, or more points than needed to reach zero, he has 'busted.' His score reverts to the score required prior to the beginning of his turn." Busting can also be used as a tactical move. For example, if a player has left double 20 and misses, hitting a single 20, this leaves double 10. If the player then hits a single 15 with his second dart instead of double 10, leaving 5 "to split" (that is, he needs to shoot another odd number to bring the figure back to a double), he may choose to throw for a single 4 or higher to "bust" the score so he can go back to his preferred double 20 on his next turn. Remember: Any time you are left with a score of 1, zero (when not acquired by a double), or a negative number, you have busted.

Know Your Numbers

Darts author and coach Noel E. Williamson appreciated the need for people learning the game to understand the *value* of the individual numbers and combinations of singles, doubles, and triples on a dartboard. Without this basic knowledge, players who were not mathematically proficient would have problems playing and enjoying the game.

To this end, Williamson prepared a "Singles, Doubles, and Triples Combination Chart" that indicates not only the value of the double of each number, but also all other combinations from "Single and Double or One Triple" through "Three Triples (Maximum)." The only scoring areas not included in the chart are the outer bull's-eye (or outer cork), which scores 25 points, and the bulls-eye (or cork), which scores 50 points. The chart is reproduced in Appendix A with permission of Williamson's family.

Once players have familiarized themselves with the values of each of the 20 numbers and their combinations, they can move on to the more complex matter of calculating outshots—that is, the numerous combinations of two and three darts that will win a game.

Outshots

There are numerous ways to complete a game of 501 or any other "01" game.

Sure, shooting a nine-dart "perfect game" (see page 38) of 501 every time would be nice, albeit most likely impossible. Thus it is useful for everyone, especially those playing darts for the first time and those wishing to improve their outshots, to be aware of the ways in which an "01" can be finished in both two and three darts.

The highest outshot achievable in three darts is 170 (triple 20, triple 20, and bull's-eye, the bull's-eye counting as a double: double 25, or 50 points); the most spectacular outshot is 150 (three bull's-eyes). To help you learn just some of the possible outshots, I have reproduced, with the permission of David King at www.Darts501.com, an outshot chart in Appendix B. This by no means covers all the hundreds of two- and three-dart permutations for each number, but will guide you with some recommended finishes. You will eventually memorize the outshots most suitable for your own game and even come up with others. They will become second nature to you and you will not need to refer to the chart.

There are a number of scores under 170 that you may find yourself on that cannot be accomplished in three darts: 169, 168, 166, 165, 163, 162, and 159. Remember them. To leave yourself any of these scores when your opponent is close behind (or, worse still, ahead of you) will automatically give him at least another three darts to finish his game. Avoid these "bogey numbers" at all costs.

There is also one number under 101 that you cannot shoot out in two darts. This bogey number is 99. So be warned. If you have a manageable outshot remaining, mentally check before you throw your first dart what score might leave you 99. If you leave that number, it will be impossible for you to finish the game with your remaining two darts. In the early days of darts, this situation gave rise to the expression, "Ninety-nine never won a game."

Learn the outshots and mold the possibilities to your own preferences and style of play—and remember those bogey numbers. If you don't, they could lose you the game.

❦

DARTING NIRVANA:
THE PERFECT GAME

Imagine starting a game of 501. Three visits to the dartboard later—nine darts in total—and you claim victory. That's a darts player's nirvana: the perfect game of 501. Although there are other ways to achieve this, the most common is for a player to hit six successive triple 20s with his first two throws. This tallies 360 points and leaves the player to score 141 with his final three darts. The outshot can be done in a number of ways. For example: triple 20 (60), triple 17 (51), and double 15 (30 and gameshot).

On October 13, 1984, John Lowe achieved the most famous (and the first televised) nine-dart finish. At the MFI World Matchplay Championship in Slough, England, Lowe hit six successive triple 20s and then shot out on 141 by hitting triple 17 (51 points), triple 18 (54 points), and double 18 (36 points and gameshot). For his trouble, Lowe earned £102,000 ($165,953), which, as of this writing, is still a record amount of prize money for achieving a nine-darter. In *Old Stoneface*, Lowe's autobiography, he described his achievement as "two and a half minutes of magic."

In 1990, Paul Lim, the number one–ranked U.S. player, became the first darts player to hit the perfect game in the Embassy World Professional Darts Championship. His choice of outshot for his final three darts was triple 20 (60), triple 19 (57), and double 12 (24 and gameshot). His prize was £52,000 ($84,604).

For most darts players, the perfect nine-dart 501 remains a pipe dream. Not so for the pros. Nowadays, nine-darters are recorded regularly at major competitions; in fact, the prize money for doing so is either a lot less than the sums stated above or nonexistent. Because of this, John Lowe has suggested that perhaps the standard game of 501 should be increased to 701, thus setting the bar higher and increasing the "Darts Nirvana" to an impressive twelve-dart 701.

A WORD ABOUT
DARTS AVERAGES

Darts averages (the number of points scored per dart or per throw of three darts) have become increasingly important to players as a benchmark of performance and an indicator to up-and-coming players of the kind of scores they must attain if they are to be successful.

Up until the early 1970s, averages were rarely kept; all that mattered was to record the name of the winner and (possibly) the runner-up. Since the late 1970s, averages per dart and per three darts have been kept and have become an increasingly important tool in comparing the abilities of players. To be able to stay in a match in the 70s and 80s with, say, either John Lowe or Eric Bristow, the opponent would have to score between 28 and 32 points per dart or 84 and 96 for every three darts thrown.

Since then, the bar has been raised time and time again, and the man who continuously resets the standard on the professional darts circuit today is Phil "The Power" Taylor. (See page 134.) Taylor regularly averages in excess of 110 per throw (37 per dart) and at the time of this writing is practicing hard to raise the bar even higher to 120—or more!

At the bar level, dart averages are not as important because the game is often played as a social activity and not always as a serious match that must be won at all costs. However, to stay in most leagues the least a player should score on a consistent basis is 20–25 per dart (60–75 in three darts). To finish a game of 501 at that level in fifteen to eighteen darts is standard, but in the professional game the target is always ten to eleven darts or the "darting nirvana"—the perfect nine-darter.

In cricket, where three-dart averages have little meaning, the perfect game can be completed in just eight darts, closing all six triples (20 through 15) with the first six darts and then either a single bull's-eye, a double bull, or two double bull's-eyes with the remaining two darts.

CRICKET

Though 501 is the gold standard darts game worldwide, cricket is the most popular game in local bars and national tournaments in the United States. In the UK, it's called tactics and should not be confused with the British game of cricket, which is discussed in chapter 4. On occasion, elsewhere, it is called Mickey Mouse. Whatever it is called, this is one of the most adversarial darts games.

It is an intriguing and strategic game for two or more players or teams. The rules are very easy to learn, but to actually master the game takes time and experience. The aim of the game is for each player or team to hit three of the numbers 20, 19, 18, 17, 16, and 15 and the bull's-eye and to accrue as high a score as possible by opening and closing those numbers (also known as "owning").

"Closing" a number or the bull's-eye is achieved when a player or team has hit three of that number or bull (either two double bulls or a single and a double bull). The first player or team to "close" is said to "own" that number, which basically means that they (and they alone) can score on that number as many points as they can before the opposition hits three of that number, or bull, and thus closes the target completely.

For example, if the first player scores triple 20, single 20, and triple 18, then he has closed the 20, scored 20 points (for hitting the single 20), and closed the 18. He can now accumulate scores on 20s and 18s; the opposition cannot score on those numbers, but can shoot for them in order to close them down completely. No player can score on any number after it has been closed by both sides.

In cricket, the triple of the numbers 20 through 15 are all-important, as three of each number are required in order to close it. Thus, a good darts player can quickly close numbers in his team's favor. Clearly, three of a number can be achieved in other ways, such as a single and a double or three singles, but this effectively wastes darts. Hitting a triple of the number with the first dart will enable the player to either score on that number (if only closed by him) or try to hit another triple to close another number.

The winner is the individual or team that closes all seven targets first *and* has equal or more points than its opponent. There is no specified order in which these numbers need to be scored. In fact, this is all part of the strategy of cricket. However, bearing in mind that the purpose is to accumulate as many points as possible before your opponent closes the number (that is, each individual or team has scored three of the number), it is common to start with the 20 first when throwing for the numbers.

The perfect start to any game of cricket is a "round of nine," whereby the player hits triple 20, triple 19, and triple 18 with his first three darts. The perfect game can be completed in just eight darts, closing all six triples (20 through 15) with the first six darts and then either a single bull's-eye and a double bull or two double bull's-eyes with the remaining two darts.

The aim is to beat your opponent by closing all the target numbers, yet you must ensure that when you do your score is higher or equal to his. (There is a variation of cricket where no points are actually scored and the winner is simply the first individual or team to close down all the numbers.)

In the standard game of cricket, points *are* scored, so the game becomes one of strategy; each individual or team is directly influenced by what the other individual or team is doing. As the game progresses, each player must make a decision as to whether he throws for points on the numbers he has already closed or throw for numbers that have yet to be closed. This is the fascination of cricket. One foul dart (a dart that misses the intended target) can turn the game on its head and hand the advantage over to the opposition.

So many elements play a part in cricket that one game is never the same as another. Each game will require different tactics. In a team situation, tactics will often be discussed in between throws, but such discussions must not be so long as to interfere with the rhythm of the match or of your opponent(s).

Here are some fundamental things to keep in mind about cricket:

1. Throwing first can be an overwhelming advantage, particularly in a game where competitors are equally matched. Who throws first can be decided by the toss of a coin. However, it's preferable to have a "bull-up" between individual opponents or two selected members from each team.

2. When you're ahead on points, you should usually shoot to close the remaining numbers, especially those which your opponent already is scoring on. However, it depends on how far ahead you are. A prime tactic is to keep a comfortable points gap between you and your opponent, but not to become a "point monger" (see Appendix C).

3. When you or your team are behind on points, you have to choose whether to throw for points on the numbers only you have closed, close other numbers that the opposition has yet to close (and then score points), or close the numbers that the opposition is scoring on. Consider the situation *very* carefully.

4. Toward the end of the game, it is crucial for you or your team to stay ahead on points. So often the game ends with attention focusing on the bull's-eye (the target that tends to be initially ignored by many players), everything else being entirely closed down.

At the beginning of a game, the scoreboard for cricket looks like this:

PLAYER A		PLAYER B
	20	
	19	
	18	
	17	
	16	
	15	
	B	

Here is the standard method of indicating scoring in cricket:

/ indicates a hit on a segment.

X indicates two hits on a segment.

O indicates that the third hit has been achieved and thus the segment is closed.

Sample Cricket Game

This simple game assumes an above-average skill level for both participants.

First turn: Player A hits three 20s and closes the 20. Player B hits a triple 20 and two 19s. The 20 is now completely closed to both players. At this point, the scoreboard looks like this:

PLAYER A		PLAYER B
O	20	O
	19	X
	18	
	17	
	16	
	15	
	B	

Second turn: Player A hits a single 19, a triple 19, and a single 18. Thus, the 19 is now closed and 19 points are scored. Player B hits a triple 18, shoots his second dart at the 18, too, but unfortunately misses, while his third dart hits a single 19. These darts close both 18 and 19.

PLAYER A		PLAYER B
19		
O	20	O
O	19	⊗
/	18	O
	17	
	16	
	15	
	B	

Third turn: Player A hits two 18s and a 17. The 18 is closed. Player B hits a triple 17, a single 17, and then goes for the 17 again with his last dart to try to score more points, but he misses. The 17 is closed and 17 points are scored. This is how the scoreboard looks after the third turn:

PLAYER A		PLAYER B
19		**17**
O	20	O
O	19	⊗
⊘	18	O
/	17	O
	16	
	15	
	B	

Fourth turn: Player A hits two 17s and a single 16. The 17 is closed. Player B hits only a single 16 with his three darts. The position is therefore:

PLAYER A		PLAYER B
19		**17**
◯	**20**	◯
◯	**19**	⊗
⊘	**18**	◯
⊘	**17**	◯
/	**16**	/
	15	
	B	

Fifth turn: Player A hits two 16s and a triple 15. The 16 and 15 are closed. Player B hits two bull's-eyes, attempting to close the bull's-eye and score points.

PLAYER A		PLAYER B
19		**17**
◯	**20**	◯
◯	**19**	⊗
⊘	**18**	◯
⊘	**17**	◯
⊘	**16**	/
◯	**15**	
	B	✕

Sixth turn: Player A hits one bull's-eye and a single 15, therefore scoring 15 points. Player shoots for the bull's-eye with all three darts and hits a double bull. The bull's-eye is closed and 25 points are scored.

PLAYER A		PLAYER B
1̶8̶		1̶7̶
34		42
◯	20	◯
◯	19	⊗
⊘	18	◯
⊘	17	◯
⊘	16	/
◯	15	
/	B	⊗

Seventh turn: Player A hits one bull's-eye in two attempts and one 16. Sixteen points are scored. Player B attempts the bull's-eye on all three darts and misses.

PLAYER A		PLAYER B
1̶8̶		1̶7̶
3̶4̶		42
50		
◯	20	◯
◯	19	⊗
⊘	18	◯
⊘	17	◯
⊘	16	/
◯	15	
✕	B	⊗

Eighth turn: Player A hits one bull's-eye and wins the game.

PLAYER A		PLAYER B
~~19~~		~~17~~
~~34~~		42
50		
◯	20	◯
◯	19	⊗
⊘	18	◯
⊘	17	◯
⊘	16	/
◯	15	
⊗	B	⊗

4

OTHER DARTS GAMES

There is no reason on earth why darts players of any skill level should find themselves saying, "I'm bored with 501 and cricket and there's nothing else to do." This chapter will introduce you to just a fraction of the hundreds of alternative darts games that can liven up your practice routine and provide some fun, relaxing competition.

Alternative games tend to fall into one of three distinct categories. First, they are darting variations of existing sports, games, or pastimes. Second, there are the original darts games, devised to maintain interest in darts over and above the standard "01" games; and, third, there are those games, usually derivative of existing games, that are played simply for fun and defy proper explanation. Whatever alternative game you choose, every one requires skill and is extremely competitive.

The games cited below are selected examples and it is impossible to record all the variations of these games, as rules may vary from one place to the next. Thus one set of rules has been applied to each game. To include all possible permutations of rules for all the alternative games would have required a book in itself. All darters be advised: When taking on locals on their home turf, make sure that you are absolutely clear about the rules before play commences.

Note: In all games, unless otherwise specified, each side takes turns, with an individual or team member throwing three darts on a turn.

GAMES DERIVED FROM
OTHER GAMES OR SPORTS

Baseball

It did not take long for the national pastime of baseball to be transferred onto the dartboard. The game can be played on-on-one or as a team.

If you play as a team (as you would in the real thing), this can generate a great atmosphere, as the teams (of varying skill levels) seek those runs. Also, as in real baseball there are nine innings. These innings are indicated by utilizing the numbers 1, 2, 3, 4, 5, 6, 7, 8, and 9. Those numbers are written down the left-hand side of the scoreboard like this (the scoreboard in this example being drawn up for two individual players).

	PLAYER A	PLAYER B
1		
2		
3		
4		
5		
6		
7		
8		
9		

The aim of the game is, of course, to score as many runs as possible during each team's innings. To score a run, each individual or team member shoots for each number in turn, 1–9. Only darts that hit the target count as runs.

Runs are scored according to what each player achieves; that is, if he hits a single of the number, he has scored one run; a double scores two runs; and a triple three runs. The triple is naturally the best segment to shoot for, and thus a perfect individual inning or turn would be three triples of the same number (nine runs). The player or team with the most runs at the end of the nine innings is declared the winner. In the case of a tied match, extra innings can be played, continuing on with the 10 segment (as the tenth inning) and so on until there is a clear winner.

Let's take a look at an example of this "national" game.

First inning: Players shoot for 1.

Player A shoots his three darts at the number 1 and hits a triple, but misses with his other two darts. He scores 3 runs. Player B hits two single 1s and a double, scoring 4 runs.

Second inning: Players shoot for 2.

Player A hits a single 2 and a triple, scoring 4 runs. Player B misses the target (2) completely and so scores no runs. The scores are registered cumulatively, so after two innings the scoreboard will look like this:

	PLAYER A	PLAYER B
1	3	4
2	7	4
3		
4		
5		
6		
7		
8		
9		

Third inning: Players shoot for 3.

Player A hits two doubles 3s and misses with his other dart, hitting four runs to add to his running total. Player B shoots three triple threes, for nine runs.

Fourth inning: Players shoot for 4.

Player A hits two single 4s and one triple, scoring five runs, while player B hits one single and one double to earn three runs. Thus, after four innings the game is as close as it can be.

	PLAYER A	PLAYER B
1	3	4
2	7	4
3	11	13
4	16	16
5		
6		
7		
8		
9		

This game would then continue until all nine innings had been played and the player with the highest number of runs was declared the winner.

Bowls

Bowls, a game in which wooden balls are rolled down carefully manicured lawns at a small white round ball (the "jack") situated at the end of the "rink," is easily transferable to the dartboard.

The art of the normal game of bowls is to try to roll your bowls closer to the jack than your opponent does. The process in darts bowls is very similar, whereby the bull's-eye is the "jack" and players throw their three darts to see who can throw nearest and score up to three points. This game is best played by two people or a maximum of four. More than that and the area around the "jack" becomes very crowded with numerous darts already on the "rink"—that is, on the dartboard—and these may well be damaged by incoming projectiles.

The aim of the game is to be the first player to reach an agreed-on number of points, usually ten. One point is scored for each dart that is nearer to the center than that of your opponents. Thus if Player A scores a bull's-eye and two outer bulls and Player B's darts are all outside the bull, then Player A is credited with a maximum three points. However, in this example, if Player B also managed to hit an outer bull, then Player A scores only one point (for the bull's-eye). Points are only awarded for those darts belonging to the player whose dart is closest to the center. The first player to reach ten points is the winner. It is important to note that if two opponents each has a dart in the single bull and no player has hit a double bull then this is considered a tie, even if one player's dart is closer to the double bull than the other.

In real bowls, the jack is never in the same place. So, too, can it be in darts bowls. Instead of using the bull's-eye all the time, nominate a double or a triple to be the jack.

English Cricket

Although the English game of cricket continues to mystify and bemuse Americans, its popularity in many other countries (mainly those that used to be part of the British Empire) knows no bounds. Thus it is logical that, early on, British darts players created a game of cricket for the dartboard. However, players outside the UK do *not* need to understand the complexities of English cricket to enjoy this game.

English cricket is a team game with eleven men playing eleven men, the aim being to knock out the opposing side ("wickets") for the least amount of score ("runs") in the shortest possible time. The darts game of English cricket has exactly the same aim. Provided that both English cricket teams have equal numbers, the actual number of players per side does not matter. If there's a spare player, he could be employed as an impartial umpire or, better still, the "chalker" or marker of the game.

Teams are often chosen by argument and bickering (rather like the English national cricket squad), but usually all the players throw one dart each at the bull's-eye and the half of the players whose darts are nearest the center comprise one team and the other half whose darts are farthest away from the bull become the opposition. Each team elects a captain and then a few moments are set aside to enable teams to come up with a team name.

The captain's primary role is to determine the order in which his team will play and to ensure that each member of the team throws in the correct sequence. His first task is to throw one dart for the bull's-eye against the opposing captain. The one whose dart is nearer the center then decides whether his team will "bowl" or "bat." Once this is decided, the name of the team to bat and ten wickets are written on the scoreboard:

CARPENTERS
| | | | |
| | | | |

The team that is to "bowl" throws first, with one team member taking a turn and hitting as many bull's-eyes as possible, each outer bull scoring one "wicket" and every bull's-eye two wickets. As each wicket is struck, a wicket is deleted from the scoreboard.

Now, a member of the batting team throws his three darts to score the highest possible score. All points scored over 40 are credited as "runs." If a team member scores 40 or fewer, no score has been achieved. Thus if a player hits triple 20, single 19, and single 3 for a total of 82, the runs scored are 42. These are then scored on the scoreboard, like this:

CARPENTERS
ⅠⅠⅠⅠⅠ
ⅠⅠ
42

Note that, at this point in the game, the Carpenters have already lost three wickets, so the score, in cricketing parlance, is 42 for 3. Team members throw alternately until all ten wickets have been hit. The total score is recorded at the top of the scoreboard and the opposing team's name (and ten wickets) drawn on the scoreboard:

CARPENTERS 243 all out
LINCOLN'S MEN
ⅠⅠⅠⅠⅠ
ⅠⅠⅠⅠⅠ

The roles are then reversed: The Carpenters become the bowling side and Lincoln's Men the batting side. The game is then played until either Lincoln's Men are all bowled out for less than the score attained by the Carpenters (243), in which case the Carpenters are declared the winners, or Lincoln's Men exceed the score of 243, in which case they have won the game.

In some of the more cutthroat versions of this game, a bowler is penalized for throwing a dart beyond the triple ring—any such score is credited to the batting side. In other versions, if a member of the batting side accidentally throws a dart "off the island" (off the scoring surface of the dartboard) or hits the outer bull, his side loses a wicket. If he hits the bull's-eye, his team loses *two* wickets.

Soccer (Football)

Soccer, the sport played by millions throughout the world (where they most likely call it *football*), is easily transferred to the dartboard.

As soon as the teams have been chosen, the captains decide the order of play either by bulling up or by tossing a coin. The winning captain is deemed to have possession of the "ball." The "ball" is the bull's-eye, either the outer or inner bull counting as a "goal." While the winning captain's team is in possession of the ball, his team wants to throw for doubles—any double—around the outside of the dartboard. Each double hit scores one goal, regardless of the value of the double. Each goal is marked up on the scoreboard.

To take possession of the ball, the opposing team merely has to hit the bull's-eye. This gives the ball to their team and they can then go for doubles (goals) until the other side hits a bull's-eye and regains possession.

The first team to score ten goals is the winner.

Tic-Tac-Toe

Best played by two players, this game adopts the traditional format of the game tic-tac-toe. Whether an individual player is playing against another or it is played as a team game, one is designated as the X and the other the O.

A 3×3 grid containing nine numbers is drawn on the scoreboard. The numbers should be random, except for the middle number, which is most often the bull's-eye, since this "center square" creates a lot of winning options. The other numbers can be determined randomly by each player using his weak hand to throw four times at the board. Here's a sample grid:

14	4	8
20	50	6
17	13	19

The purpose of the game is to be the first player to "own" a straight line of three numbers, across, down, or diagonally. To own a number, a player must hit the number's double segment. (An even more challenging variant requires hitting a triple of the given number, except, of course, for the bull's-eye.) As players hit the required doubles of the given numbers or the bull's-eye, the appropriate X or O replaces the number. A game in progress might look like this:

14	O	X
O	X	X
O	13	19

In this example, both players still have a chance of winning the game, O by striking double 14—or double 13 *and* double 19, while X could finish the game with double 19.

As with the original game, tic-tac-toe can result in stalemate. If, in the example above, X hits double 13, then double 14 to block O, then only X can win. But then O hits double 19 to bring the game to a close with no outright winner. The final scoreboard will look like this:

X	O	X
O	X	X
O	X	O

An extension of the principle of tic-tac-toe can be found in a game known as three in a row. Here, the grid is enlarged to sixteen spaces and the numbers 1 to 16 drawn in:

1	2	3	4
5	6	7	8
9	10	11	12
13	14	15	16

(17)

The first number to be used in the second stage of the game is written to one side of the grid, merely as a reminder: in this case, 17.

In this game the aim is still to score on doubles and to gain three in a row either vertically, horizontally, or diagonally, but it is played by teams of two or more. This adds spice to the game because levels of individual skill vary enormously, as does the degree of luck when shooting for particular doubles.

So let's say that Harold and Maude (HM) are playing Sid and Nancy (SN). Both teams are playing well and their success so far is recorded by replacing the number with their initials. Here's the state of play:

SN	HM	3	4
5	SN	HM	8
SN	SN	11	SN
13	14	15	16

The game is under the control of Sid and Nancy. They can win on their next throw with double 3, double 5, double 11, or double 14. Harold and Maude cannot win on one dart.

Let's say that the game progresses a while longer and then Sid and Nancy take the game as follows:

SN	HM	**SN**	4
5	**SN**	HM	8
SN	SN	HM	SN
13	14	15	16

Sid and Nancy have won the game with three in a row diagonally but Harold and Maude insist on another game. If agreed, all the letters SN and HM are removed from the scoreboard and replaced by the numbers from 17 to 20 plus the bull's-eye (50). Any other remaining spaces are filled with numbers beginning again from the number 1. Thus, at the start of the second game, the grid looks like this:

17	18	19	4
5	20	50	8
1	2	3	4
13	14	15	16

(5)

Note that the next number, 5, is marked at the side of the grid, just in case there is a third and deciding game. Note, too, that there are now two 4s and 5s in the grid. If the game is played over a long period during an evening, it is not uncommon for a number to appear twice or more times within the same grid. If this occurs, as it has with 4 in the example above, and the player hits a double 4, then he only claims one of those numbers, choosing the one that works to his best advantage.

Shove Ha'penny

In years gone by, the shove ha'penny board jockeyed for popularity with darts in English pubs. Nowadays, shove ha'penny boards are rare and are brought out for play for nostalgic purposes only.

Darts shove ha'penny is similar to American cricket, except that it lacks point scoring and has one unique twist.

Once teams have been decided, the numbers 1 to 9 are written down the scoreboard. (Sometimes the bull's-eye is also included.) The purpose is to close each number by hitting it three times (doubles count as two points and triples as three). Thus, halfway through a game the scoreboard might look something like this:

BOOK LOVERS		SPORTS FANATICS
III	1	I
III	2	III
II	3	I
II	4	
III	5	
II	6	III
I	7	II
	8	II
I	9	I

Here's the twist: Any extra scores you make on a number you have already closed are transferred across to your opponent. Using the example above, if the Book Lovers accidentally hit a triple 5, those three hits will count for Sports Fanatics and close out the 5 for them. Or if Sports Fanatics throw a single 9 followed by a triple 9 (when undoubtedly aiming for a single), the two extra 9 hits will go to the Book Lovers and close out the 9 for them as well. In this example, neither of the teams requires any more 2s and, if any more are scored, the shot has been wasted.

The first team to close out all nine numbers is the winner. *Note:* The winning point must be thrown by the winning side and not result from a wayward dart thrown by the opposition. All the other points can be gifts from your opponent—just not the winning one.

OTHER ALTERNATIVE GAMES

The games in this section have sprung from simply playing darts and owe their origins, as far as can be ascertained, from no other existing game.

High and Low Boxes

High boxes is a popular game in the United States. It can be played by any number of players from two on up. Like many of these alternative darts games, the more the merrier. This game is often played with a small side wager of perhaps a dollar per player, with the eventual winner taking the pot.

The purpose of the game is for each player to beat the score achieved by the player who throws before him. (In low boxes the players have to score less than the preceding player.)

The order of play is decided by all players throwing one dart at the bull's-eye. If two or more players hit the center, then those players throw at the bull again. The final starting order is then marked down the left-hand side of the scoreboard. Along the top of the scoreboard is written "Round 1," "Round 2," and so on, so that, in this example of a game played by four players, the starting position looks like this:

	ROUND 1	ROUND 2	ROUND 3	ROUND 4
Glen				
Jane				
Holly				
Bob				

As Bob is last on the list, having been farthest away from the bull's-eye, it is his job to determine the starting score for Glen to beat. Bob must throw two darts *at the same time* with his usual throwing hand. This is called "splashing."

Let's say that Bob scored a single 17 and a single 9 with his "splashed" darts. The total number (26) is written in the top left-hand corner of the scoreboard, just above Glen's name. This is the score Glen must beat.

If a player fails to beat (not equal, but exceed) the previous player's score using *all three darts*, then an "x" is placed next to his name. In many cases, these attempts are known as "lives." Players have only three lives, and each "lost life" is indicated by an "x." This means that a player can only miss his target score three times; after that, they are out of the game. Whatever a player scores serves as the new score for the next player to beat. Play continues in rotation until all but one player has earned three x's. The one remaining player is the winner.

To illustrate high boxes, here's a game where three rounds have been completed:

26	ROUND 1	ROUND 2	ROUND 3	ROUND 4
Glen ✕	31	35	40	
Jane	45	40	41	
Holly	60	52	60	
Bob ✕✕✕	23	45	43	

At this stage, Bob has been having a bad night and is, sadly, out of the game. He was unable to beat Holly's scores in any of the rounds. At the beginning of round 3, Glen failed to beat the score of 45 that Bob left at the end of round 2, so he has one "x." The game will continue (without Bob) until a winner is determined.

Note: Change the order of players after each game to even out the competition. Bob doesn't want to be stuck behind Holly all night!

Some players feel that low boxes is the more frustrating of the two "boxes" games, as it seems more difficult to continuously hit low scores. With high boxes, a lucky triple can be very useful, but in low boxes one errant triple can easily gain the player a very high score and an "x"— while making life much easier for the following player.

In some variations of these games, players are penalized with an "x" if they hit a non-scoring part of the dartboard or fail to have a dart land in the dartboard at all. This is especially necessary in the case of low boxes; otherwise, players would just throw their darts into the ground, scoring zero all the time, and there would be no point to the game!

Compass Points

Compass points is played more for practice than competition. It can be played either north to south (the 20 segment down to the 3 segment) or east to west (the 6 segment across to the 11 segment).

If you choose to shoot "north to south," you must hit the following targets *in sequence*: the double 20, "big" single 20, triple 20, "small" single 20, outer bull, bull's-eye, "small" single 3, triple 3, "big" single 3, finishing on double 3. You must recall where you left off at the end of each turn or mark it down on the scoreboard. For "east to west," the task is the same but from right to left, double 6 through to double 11.

The first player to complete the trek wins.

Doubles Killer

Doubles killer is sometimes simply known as killer. To win the game, players have to "kill" all their opponents.

Players begin the game with an agreed-upon number of "lives" (usually five). Each player has his own personal number (a double), which is determined by throwing a dart at the dartboard with the wrong hand. (If a dart lands outside the scoring area or misses the dartboard entirely, then the player must throw again.) If two or more players hit the same number, they throw again until their numbers are different.

The order of play is then settled by "bulling up." Once that is decided, the players' names are marked on the scoreboard with their numbers in parentheses and their starting allotment of lives. At the start of a game, the scoreboard will look like this:

Wilma (14)	IIIII
Barney (10)	IIIII
Angel (18)	IIIII
Sam (11)	IIIII

In order to become a "killer," each player must first hit his own target. In this case, Angel must hit double 18 before she attains "killer" status. As soon as Angel becomes a killer, she can set about killing off her opponents by shooting for their doubles. Each double removes one life. If the player hits his own double by mistake, he loses his killer status and must hit his double again to regain it. Here is a game in progress:

Wilma (14)	IIIII
Barney (10)	III
Angel (18)	II
Sam (11)	IIIII K

The "K" at the end of Sam's lives indicates that he is the only killer at the moment and that he seems to be paying more attention to "killing" Barney and Angel than to killing Wilma. This is probably because his double (11) is right next door to Wilma's double (14) on a dartboard and if Sam hit his own double when trying to hit Wilma's, he would lose his killer status. However, that leaves Wilma time to hit her own double and perhaps Sam will find that Wilma is more adventurous and will try to kill him off.

The winner is the last player left standing.

For a shorter version of the game, each player has three lives rather than five. For novice darters, the game can be played by scoring on single numbers, rather than doubles.

Little and Large

Little and large is a very popular alternative darts game loosely based on killer but demanding (perhaps) more skill and determination. In this game, the target segment changes over and over again and players have to work harder to preserve their "lives" than in any other darts game.

This game is also known as "follow on" because the players simply follow each other trying to hit the segment of the dartboard that has been left by the previous player—and that's all there is to it!

Each player has five "lives." To begin, the names of all the players are written vertically down the scoreboard in a random order with five lives next to each one:

Doug	IIIII
Lynda	IIIII
Maureen	IIIII
Arthur	IIIII
Ian	IIIII
Henry	IIIII

The last player on the list—in this case, Henry, as indicated in the above example—throws a single dart with his wrong hand and wherever it lands in the scoring area of the dartboard becomes the target for the player at the top of the list (Doug). If Henry misses the scoring area completely, he must throw again with his wrong hand until he leaves a score.

Let's say, for example, that Henry is lucky and hits a double 5. That is Doug's target. Two single 5s do not count. Doug has five lives (15 darts) in which to hit the double 5. If he fails to hit that target with his first three darts, then he loses one life, which is erased from the scoreboard. If he fails with the next three darts, another life is lost.

However, if Doug manages to hit the double 5 with, say, the second dart of his third turn, he then has *one dart* to set the target for the next player, Lynda. Whatever he scores with that last dart (provided it is within the scoring area) is the target for Lynda. If he fails to hit the target or the dart bounces out, then Doug loses another life. In that case, he then has three darts with which to achieve a target for Lynda. With darts to spare, some players go for a difficult double with their first dart (perhaps double 3 or double 11), but wherever the dart lands in the scoring area will be the target for the next player.

All doubles and triples count, as do inner and outer bull's-eyes. The game is called little and large because all 20 scoring sections have a "little" segment (between the outer bull and the triple ring) and a "large" segment (between the triple ring and the double ring). Thus, if Doug leaves Lynda a single 1 between the outer bull and the triple, Lynda can only score this "little" 1 and not a triple, double, or "large" 1.

If Lynda fails to hit a little 1 with her five attempts, then she has lost all her lives and is out of the game. After Lynda, it is up to the next player (Maureen) to hit the little 1. If she does, then whatever she leaves with her next dart is the target for Arthur. If Maureen fails, then the little 1 remains the target for Arthur.

If a player finds himself with only one dart to set the target for the next player, it is usually recommended to shoot for the bull's-eye. If the player hits it (or the outer bull), that could cost the following players a life or two, and if he misses then it *should* leave a "little" number.

Thus, the game is played out until only one player remains and is declared the winner.

In the less serious version of this game, the closed-loop areas contained in some of the numbers around the dartboard (4, 6, 8, 9, 10, 14, 16, 18, 19, 20) or even the letters of the dartboard trade name (for example W-I-N-M-A-U) are deemed legitimate targets. Thus, if a player, having hit the required target, is feeling particularly evil (and is especially skilled), he can leave a "loopy 8" or the "I" of WINMAU. In the former case, there are, of course, two loops, so the following player must hit the right loop to progress in the game!

This sociable game demands a great deal of skill and, at times, more than a little luck. It can be further enlivened by a small side wager—say $1 per person.

Fives

Derived from playing darts on the old fives dartboard, this game of the same name combines accurate dart-throwing with a certain degree of mental agility. Fives can be played by any number of players and makes an excellent team game.

The idea of fives is for each player to throw three darts and make certain that the total scored with those three darts is divisible by five. If so, then points are scored for each "five" scored. For example, a total of 20 scores four points (20 divided by five), a total of 35 scores seven points (35 divided by five), and so on. The usual target score is either 51 points or 101 points.

Any three-dart total that is not divisible by five is deemed as "no score" and therefore no points are awarded. If a dart bounces off the wire, falls out of the dartboard, or misses the target area entirely, the whole score for that turn is void.

The game is mostly played on two specific areas of the dartboard—the area occupied by the 5 and 20 and that occupied by the 15 and 10. If a player can keep within those areas, then points will be scored every time. However, the mental agility comes in when there's a stray dart. For example, the first dart goes into the 20 but the second hits the 1 segment. That's 21 scored—not divisible by five—so the player can now aim for triple 18 (54), which will yield the highest number of points from that position (75 ÷ 5 = 15). Or one could play it more conservatively and just try to hit a single, such as 4, 9, 14, or 19.

To win the game, a player must score 51 or 101 *exactly*. Thus, if he is on 48 points, the number of points required to win is three. If he then hits a total of 20, which is four points—one too many—he has "bust" and his score reverts to 48 points.

Also, players must use all three darts to score the required number to win. Therefore, if a player is at 50 and needs one point to win, shooting a single five with his first dart results in a bust rather than a victory. He still has two other darts left and to throw any dart off the scoring area voids the turn. One winning sequence for a single point would be single 2, single 2, single 1.

In a variation of fives, all doubles and triples only count as one point and the bull's-eye and outer bull do not count at all.

Fox and Hound

As the name suggests, fox and hound is a "chase" game in which one player (the "fox") has to travel around the dartboard, pursued by another player (the "hound"). It is a game normally played by two players. Fortunately, there's no violent death or bloodshed in the darts version.

At the beginning of the game, a coin is tossed or the players bull-up to determine who is to play which role. The player who wins chooses whether to be the fox or the hound. The fox throws first. The aim of the game is for the fox to begin from its lair (the 20 segment), and then move in a counterclockwise direction around the dartboard, hitting each segment along the way, and then returning safely to his lair (by hitting single 20 again) without the hound catching him.

In the basic form of the game, this is done on singles only. The fox begins by throwing at a single 20 and as soon as that target is struck, he moves on to the 5 segment, then to the 12 segment, and so on. The idea, of course, is to stay ahead of the hound all the time as the two players alternate turns of three darts.

In order to give the fox a reasonable start, the hound begins at single 18 (two segments behind). If the hound catches up to the fox by reaching the fox's current number, the fox is captured. The round is over. Note the number, reverse the roles of fox and hound, and start the hunt again. The new fox wins if he makes further progress than the first fox.

If the first fox manages to stay ahead of the hound and return safely to its lair, then count the number of segments that the hound was behind. Then reverse the roles. If the second fox also returns safely to its lair, then the hound that finished its hunt with the fewest number of segments between it and the fox is declared the winner.

Those who find fox and hound too easy to play on single segments can try the more advanced version in which both the fox and the hound must score a single *and* a double of each segment before moving on. In another version, the fox must score a single and a double of each number, whereas the hound only has to score a double starting from double 18. (That sounds rather like animal cruelty!)

Halve It

In halve it, numbers—either singles, doubles, or triples—are chosen at random by the players and written down the left-hand side of the board, with players' names across the top.

The numbers are targeted in order and for only one round each. Each player gets one three-dart turn at the round's target number. However, if the number is designated as a single number, then only singles count. That is, if a player hits the double or triple of a given number, that does not count. Similarly, if the target is, say, double 8, then singles and triples of that number are invalid. If the bull's-eye is used, then only darts that strike dead center—not the outer bull—count.

The title of this game is halve it and that is exactly what happens if a player fails to score on a target number—his cumulative score is cut in half. Note that when cutting an odd number in half, the score is always rounded down, although no player can go lower than a score of 1. Here is an example of a completed game:

	Amy	Eliot	Cate	Spenser
20	20	40	60	–
18	10	58	30	54
D8	26	74	15	27
T16	13	37	7	75
15	28	52	52	90
12	40	64	76	102
D10	60	84	38	51
17	77	101	55	25
13	38	114	68	12

Eliot was a clear winner in this game. However, if the scores of two or more players are tied at the end of a game, an additional number is employed for only those players to establish a winner. If the game is still tied, then further numbers are added until a winner is determined.

Halve it can also be played where you can score singles, doubles, and triples on a given number, unless it's specified as only scoring on a double or a triple. Also, the bull's-eye is often used as the last round, which can lead to major reversals of fortune.

1,001

Many team darts games are played 1,001-up, but this particular game is not the same. This 1,001 is a team game involving endurance, as it is played over no less than *four* games. Although the idea is to win the games, to win three out of four does not necessarily mean that your team will win the overall match.

In this version, the final scores in each game count. Best played pair against pair, 1,001 involves playing four (sometimes more) games of 1,001, double in and double out. However, it is the total number of points accumulated over all four (or more) games that determines the winning team.

For each win, the successful team is awarded 1,001 points, while the losing team is given the actual points they have scored. So if the losing team had 101 points left on the scoreboard when the other team won the game, they would be awarded 900 points, the total number of points they had scored. Take our two teams in Match A below. Both teams have won two games, but the aggregate score shows that Team 2 has the larger total and has therefore won the match.

GAME	TEAM 1	TEAM 2
1	1,001	900
2	600	1,001
3	930	1,001
4	1,001	652
Total	3,532	3,554

The overall scores were very close, with only 22 points separating the teams. However, in Match B there's an unusual turn of events, as noted below:

MATCH B

GAME	TEAM 1	TEAM 2
1	1,001	968
2	1,001	997
3	1,001	873
4	546	1,001
Total	3,549	3,849

Team 1 beat Team 2 in the first three games by fairly narrow margins, but was blown away by its opponents in the fourth game. Because of the nature of this version of 1,001, Team 2 takes the match, despite having won only one game.

In the majority of darts games, doubles are vitally important and perhaps even more so in this game. The longer it takes one team to double in or double out, the longer the other side has to increase its lead or reduce its deficit and—as in Match B—take the match. The game of 1,001 is all about consistency.

Round the Clock

The aim of round the clock (also known as "round the world" or "round the board") is to strike the numbers 1 through to 20 in the fewest number of darts. Each player throws three darts in turn and tries to hit as many numbers in succession as possible (a single, double, or triple of the number counts as a hit). Each number must be struck in turn, so a player cannot progress to the number 2 unless he has hit number 1. Hitting any number out of order does not count, because the proper numerical sequence must be maintained. The first player to reach 20 wins.

English Variation of Round the Clock

In the English version of this game, the rules are different and more complicated. If a player hits a double, then he may progress further. For example, if a player is on 3 and hits a double 3, then his skill is rewarded and his next throw is for seven. This reward for hitting a double is only possible up to the number 10 when, if the double is hit, the player progresses to 20. If a single 10 is struck, then the player must continue with single numbers all the way up to 20. This is known in the game as "crawling around."

When a player reaches the 20 and hits it, he then has to finish with double 20, followed by a bull's-eye. This often allows subsequent players to catch up; thus the outcome is not predictable. In some versions of this game, two outer bulls count as "bull" to complete the game.

Scram

The object of scram is for one player the "scorer" to hit as many numbers (1 to 20) as he can to achieve the best possible total before the "stopper" hits them and prevents him from scoring on them anymore.

The players toss a coin or bull-up to decide who will have which role, either "scorer" or "stopper." The "stopper" throws first and usually aims at the three highest numbers on the dartboard. As soon as the stopper has hit a number, this becomes unavailable to the scorer. The scorer then throws his three darts and tries to accumulate as high a score as he can—all doubles and triples, counting their full value. The game then continues with the stopper and scorer throwing alternatively until the stopper has struck the last available number.

Players keep track of the progress of the game by chalking the numbers 1 to 20 on the scoreboard at the start of the game. As the stopper hits each number, that number is erased and the scorer has to throw at the remaining available numbers. The scorer's points are totaled up on the scoreboard. At the end of the game, the roles are reversed and it becomes the new scorer's task to beat the total of the first player.

In a normal game of scram, only the numbers 1 to 20 are used, but there is no reason why more experienced players should not also use the bull's-eye (50) and the outer bull (25).

Shanghai

Arguably the most popular of all alternative dart games, and one of the earliest recorded alternative games, shanghai can be played by two or more players. Although there are many variations of the game, the standard form involves using the numbers 1 to 9. These are marked down the scoreboard and the names or initials of participants are written along the top, thus indicating the order of play.

Shanghai is played in rounds. In the first round, all the players are throwing at 1; in the second round, the target is 2; and so on through 9. The aim of shanghai is not only to accumulate points (all doubles and triples, counting their full value on the appropriate number) but also, and more important, to obtain a "shanghai" shot, which is hitting the single, double, and triple of the target number in three darts. At whatever point in the game this is achieved, the game is over and the player who scored the shanghai is declared the winner. (In some versions, those who still have to throw in that round are given the chance to equal the feat and, if another shanghai is achieved, then only those players continue to play each other until a winner is declared.)

Professional darts players will insist that shanghai be achieved in the correct sequence—that is, single, double, and then triple—to count. Or some play according to rules that the final shanghai shot cannot be a single. In the usual, more casual games of shanghai, hitting the three in any order is quite acceptable.

Before the game, players may designate a certain number (or numbers) that a player must hit at least once in the appropriate round. If the player fails to hit the number, he is eliminated from the game. These crucial numbers are marked with an asterisk on the scoreboard. Here then is a game of shanghai that has reached its conclusion:

	ANN	PAT	BOB	DOUG	JEN	GLEN	LISA
1	2	1	3	4	1	2	2
2	8	3	7	6	7	8	2
3*	11	x	13	15	10	14	x
4	23	x	25	31	10	22	x
5*	43	x	45	41	x	42	x
6	49	x	81	41	x	42	x
7*	63	x	130	69	x	49	x
8	87	x	146	s	x	-	x
9*							

It begins with seven players who all manage to score on 1 and 2 and so at this point Ann and Glen are joint leaders with eight points. However, the asterisked round of number 3 claims Pat and Lisa, who missed the number with all three of their darts. As the game progresses, Jen fails to score on 5s (also asterisked) and is out of the game, while the remaining four players battle it out. By the eighth round, Bob's lead looks unassailable. However, Doug manages to pull off the upset by hitting shanghai 8s (single, double, and triple), and the S is written on the scoreboard. In order for him to continue, Glen must hit shanghai 8s. He fails to do so. The game is over. Doug is acknowledged as the winner and the ninth round is unnecessary.

FUN ADAPTATIONS
Although the games in this section are described as "fun," they still allow players to practice accuracy—especially in some areas of the dartboard that would not normally be part of their game.

Blind Killer
Blind killer is similar to doubles killer, except for one big twist: The number that a player throws at is only known to the player himself. To achieve this, someone writes the numbers 1 to 20 on separate pieces of paper and puts them all into a "hat." Each player then draws a number out of the hat, looks at it, but does not reveal the number to any of his opponents. Whatever number is on the paper is his designated double.

The names of all players are marked on the scoreboard and given five lives. Unlike doubles killer, there is no need to achieve "killer" status in any way. All players are immediately killers, but the problem is they do not know which doubles the other players own.

The players then throw their darts in turn and once five doubles of an owned number have been accrued, the player with that number fesses up, hands in his number, and takes no further part in the match.

The easiest way to keep track of the doubles is to write the numbers 1 through 20 on the scoreboard and mark them whenever a double is hit. Once a number accumulates five hits, it will either eliminate a player from the game or be revealed as a nonactive number. If you don't keep track of doubles on the scoreboard, the game then becomes a test of memory—and integrity!

As with doubles killer, the winner is the last person standing after all the others have been "killed." For a quicker game, give each player only three lives.

Hit the Dollar

No need to add hit the dollar to your practice routine, but it's a fun diversion at the end of an evening of darts.

A dollar is offered up by someone. In some cases, the person who supplies the bill charges people to play in order to cover the value of the bill—or make a little profit. Obviously, this can be done with higher denominations than a single dollar.

The dollar is opened up and pinned flat to the dartboard so that its center is directly over the bull's-eye. Then, with a piece of chalk, a line is drawn on the floor one step forward of the existing throw line and another line is drawn one step back from the line. Each player then takes a turn throwing at the dollar from each of those positions: one dart from the normal line, then one dart from the forward line, and then one from the back line. Place all three darts in the bill and the dollar is yours.

Believe me when I say that is not as easy as it sounds!

Silly Tic-Tac-Toe

To play the silly version of tic-tac-toe, the normal blank grid is drawn on the scoreboard and players are asked to "think silly." After a whole range of dubious and unusual targets have been considered, the grid might end up looking something like this:

Score 43	T3	Any Red
Bull	D11	S19
BWB	Loop	3Ws

Onlookers may scratch their heads, but come on, this is the *fun* version of the game. For example, "Score 43" means that the player must score exactly 43 using all three darts. If he does so, then his X or O takes that "square" in the grid. Any score of more or less than 43 will not earn that square. However, if the player hits more than 43 with his first two darts, he can throw his last dart at any other available target achievable in one dart. In the example, these include D11 (double 11), T3 (triple 3), Bull, or "Loop."

Loop means that the player must hit the enclosed loop of any number on the metal numbered ring that surrounds the dartboard. Going around the board clockwise from the top, 20, 18, 4, 6, 10, 19, 16, 8, 14, and 9 are all possible targets. If the player hits one of those loops, his X or O replaces Loop on the grid and he can throw any remaining darts at any other legitimate targets.

Three other terms on this sample grid need explaining. *Any Red* means that the player must hit any red segment (which, along with green, represent doubles and triples on a dartboard) to claim that square on the grid. *BWB* stands for "black, white, black." Here the player must hit, in order, a black scoring segment, then a white segment, and then another (different) black segment. Finally, *3Ws* represents "three whites" and the player must hit three different white scoring segments.

As in the standard game, the winner in this crazy version of tic-tac-toe is the first player to achieve a line of three X's or O's, vertically, horizontally, or diagonally.

The key to this game is "the sillier the better" and, while a good number of the targets seem far-fetched, it will surprise you how often players hit the Loop or BWB even as they protest that they're wasting their time.

Silly Shanghai

This fun combination of shanghai and halve it involves a similar approach to targets as shown in the silly tic-tac-toe. In addition, whenever any of the targets are missed, the existing score is halved. A completed silly shanghai scoreboard might look like this:

	PEG	JANINE	DARRELL	BEN
20	20	20	–	40
Loop	10	28	20	20
D3	16	14	26	10
Bull	8	64	76	5
Under 21	4	84	95	15
13	30	110	134	41
Any Green	15	55	182	98
Score 43	58	27	91	49

In this example, the only targets where a shanghai can be obtained are 20 and 13. (When choosing your targets, have at least one number that can produce a shanghai; no such possibility would be too silly, even in a silly shanghai game.) When a loop is hit, the player scores the value of the number;

for example, if he hits a loop of the 8 in the number 18, he scores the full eighteen points. What makes this such fun is that the lead tends to change hands over and over during the course of the game. Janine was keeping up the pace and was a threat to Darrell until she stumbled on the last two targets. Despite halving out in the last round, Darrell managed to clinch the win, and Peg, who played poorly throughout, actually squeezed into second place.

Double Ya!

Finally, in this section, a game you cannot lose.

The night has been long and friends are calling out to you to play one more game of 501. You just want to go home. However, they persist. You tell them that it would be pointless, as you can beat any of them hands down. They *still* persist, so you reluctantly agree to play them but only if, to give them a chance of beating you, you allow them to double everything they score.

They agree and from that point on you are a winner. If they double every score they obtain, how are they ever going to finish a game of 501?

These are but a few of the hundreds of games that can be played on the dartboard. For a list of books that feature more games, check out Appendix D.

5

~ IMPROVING YOUR GAME ~

Practice is by far the best way of improving your game. But there are a number of other actions that darts players can take to develop their darting skills.

Some things to consider: how you approach your game play; your personal fitness (mental and physical); how confident or nervous you feel; your temperament before, during, and after each game. There is also the question of dedication. If you are not dedicated to your sport, then chances are you will not succeed. Make the decision now to become the best player you can possibly be.

Remember that darts is fundamentally different from most games. In the majority of sports, such as football, tennis, and pool, what your opponent does and how you react are vitally important to the outcome. You can be tackled in football, outhit in tennis, and snookered in pool. In darts, you are playing against the dartboard.

THE MATHEMATICS OF DARTS

The dartboard is a complex target (see Figure 16). Thus, any darts player must familiarize himself with the position of every number to the point that, if asked, he can reel off from the top (clockwise): 20, 1, 18, 4, 13, 6, 10, 15, 2, 17, 3, 19, 7, 16, 8, 11, 14, 9, 12, and 5. Second, learn the values of each double and triple.

Darts is a mathematical game. It requires addition (adding up the score

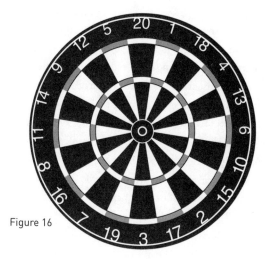

Figure 16

achieved with your three darts), subtraction (taking your score away from the total remaining), and multiplication (knowing the values of doubles and triples). Master the game's mental arithmetic and you are partway to becoming a very competent and confident player.

In a typical game, you start with 501 and work your way down to zero. Keep a close eye on your score and look for the potential outshots that are featured in Appendix B. Also, make sure you know what to shoot for next if a dart you throw does not hit its intended target. If you are not comfortable with the positions and multiples of numbers, or you do not know what score you need next, you'll be forced to pause during your turn to work out the sums. That will break your concentration and your rhythm—and could cost you the game.

Learn what doubles split down into. For example, if you go for double 10 and hit a single 10, what do you need next? Double 5. But where is that on the dartboard? Between the 12 and the 20 segments. If you hit a single 5 when going for double 5, what is your next target? Either single 1, double 2 or single 3, double 1. Knowing what each double breaks down into ensures that you are ready to adjust your game if you miss the intended target double.

Many top players prefer to finish their games on double 16 (32). That's because it's the only number on the dartboard that, if you miss it and hit the single, splits down into an even number no less than four times, from double 16 to double 8 (16), to double 4 (8), double 2 (4), and finally to double 1 (2). Each miss affords you a shot at a double with the next dart. However, if your target is double 19, what happens if you miss it? Missing double 19 (38) would leave you an odd number (19). In that case, you would have no choice but to shoot your next dart at an odd number (17, 15, 13, 11, 9, 7, 5, 3, or 1) in order to "take the odd off" and give yourself another chance at a double. Some professional players like to finish on double 20 (40). This number splits down into an even number 20 (double 10) and then again to 10 (double 5), but another miss leaves a single 5.

In time, the math in darts will become second nature to you and you will be planning your game before you even throw your first dart.

PRACTICE, PRACTICE, AND MORE PRACTICE

Practice is the only way to succeed in any sport. It is the essence of darts. When once accused by a defeated opponent of winning by "lucky darts," the English professional darts player Bob Anderson responded, "Do you know what? The more I practice, the luckier I get."

Schedule specific time for practice during the week—and stick to the schedule. Build the sessions into your normal week by taking into account work and family commitments. Some players may find that half an hour's practice every other day works fine, while more serious players might look to scheduling in an hour or two every day. Some professionals spend five or more hours a day honing their skills.

Whatever you decide to do, you will not arrive at the top level of darts unless you count your practice sessions in hours rather than minutes.

Work out your personal requirements based on your current level of play (which will always need improvement) and where you want to be in the future (the best player in the local bar, a tournament-level competitor, or perhaps even a pro). In addition, serious darts players practice not just against the dartboard at home but also in their local bar or club against quality competition. How else can you gauge your progress? Playing against first-class opponents will improve your game and, eventually, your self-confidence.

Basic Training

Your practice should not merely comprise throwing at high-scoring numbers (such as triple 20 or the bull's-eye). Sure, it's necessary to spend time practicing on the "red bit" and the "cork," but you must become proficient in every scoring area of the dartboard.

Begin by throwing three darts at each of the numbers in numerical order and record how many darts it takes you to hit each number 1 to 20 (a single, a double, or a triple counting as a hit). When you are able to hit all twenty numbers in less than twenty-five darts, move on to the next stage. Begin to practice on doubles of each number. This is much more difficult, but you must persevere. Doubles are vitally important, as you always need one to complete an "01" game. In time, you will develop favorite doubles, such as "double top" (double 20), double 18, or double 16. Remember: If you split your double, you must be prepared for the next double that it breaks down to; in these examples, namely: double 10, double 9, or double 8.

Concentrate on the "madhouse"—double 1. Early on, you will find that many of your games end up here. Often your opponent will end up there too, and the game may go on interminably, if you are both afraid of it. Don't be afraid! Don't be afraid of *any* double. They are all the same distance away from the throw line.

The same is true of the triples, and it is these segments that can earn players the greatest number of points as 501 is reduced to zero. Learn the position of the important high-scoring triples and concentrate (as the top players do) on the triple 20. However, this should not be to the exclusion of the other triples, especially triple 10 and above.

Some Practice Games

Let's be realistic: Practice *is* boring, so vary your routine as best you can. The following games concentrate on specific areas of the dartboard, assist in grouping, and generally improve your skills. Use them to make your practice sessions more lively.

51

This provides excellent practice on doubles.

Write the number *51* on the top of your scoreboard. Throw three darts at the double segments of each number, beginning at double 1. For each double you score, add the value of that double to your total. If you miss the double with all three darts, *deduct* the value of that double from your score. So, if you miss double 1 completely, your score becomes 49, but if you hit two double 1s, your score becomes 55 and so on.

While there is no particular significance in selecting the number 51 (which has traditionally always been utilized in this game), it does mean that if a player misses his doubles, he is soon out of the game. Thus, those just starting out with darts are warned that failure to hit any doubles will mean that your score will fall below zero at double 7. However, practice this on a regular basis and you will see your scores increasing and you will become proficient at hitting those doubles. (For a novice, a good score is around 100–150, and for a proficient darts player 200–300.)

As a variation, increase the number to 101 and play the same game, but with triples. Failure to hit any triples will leave you below zero at triple 8.

Middle for Diddle

Although this game first appeared in print in Noel E. Williamson's 1968 book *Darts,* as Williamson admitted at the time, it had been played in various forms for many years.

As the name suggests, middle for diddle focuses on the bull's-eye and the outer bull. Although it can be played as a competitive game, it fits ideally into any practice routine.

Playing from a 501 start, once any double has been hit, the player shoots only at the bull's-eye (50 points) and the outer bulls (25 points) until arriving at a finishing double. Until you reach that last double, nothing outside the area of the bull's-eye or outer bull counts for score. To complete the game, you must shoot out on the remaining double, which is always double 13.

Middle for diddle can be played "straight in" without a starting double.

Straight-In 101

Straight-in 101 is ideal for general practice and affords you the chance of shooting out from the start. There is usually no need to record each throw as the calculation of scores can be done inside your head. (However, if in doubt, mark it down on the scoreboard.)

The aim is simply to shoot out on 101 in as few darts as possible. It is possible in two darts (triple 17 and bull's-eye) or in three (for example, single 17, triple 18, double 15).

This game improves both your shooting ability and your mental arithmetic. When you are confident enough with 101, progress to 201.

Ten Up

Back in the 1980s, World Darts Champion John Lowe recommended ten up as ideal practice on the triple 20. The idea is to concentrate the mind on that all-important "red bit." You only score points if you hit it.

All three darts must land in the 20 segment. Only scores of 100 or more count, and each score must include one or more triples. Scoring 100 with two double 20s and a single 20 won't cut it; the focus of the game is the triple. Award yourself one point for each triple 20 scored—but only if you've notched 100 points or more and *all* three darts have landed in the 20 segment. The idea is to achieve ten points in the shortest possible time. Record how many darts it takes you each time you play and see your skills on the "red bit" develop.

Rewards
This is not a game, merely a method of encouraging yourself to improve. When you manage to beat a previous best in practice, reward yourself with your favorite sandwich or drink. In fact, set it up in view so that you can see it while you are practicing. But play fair and only give yourself the prize if it is rightfully deserved. No cheating!

The Practice Environment
In chapter 1, we discussed setting up your darts court at home so that it resembles as closely as possible a standard darts area found in any bar or club.

Let's assume that you play well in your private practice environment. The secret is then to step outside your cozy, home-based darts court and transfer those skills to a different—possibly unknown, possibly hostile—playing environment. It's a common lament among losing darts players: "I don't understand it. I was playing great in practice." This failure comes down to a player's inability to adapt to unfamiliar environments.

As Ivan Brackin and William Fitzgerald pointed out in their book *All About Darts*, "Succeeding outside the warmth of one's own environment against unknown players of unknown skill is an experience that molds future champions." In other words, the ability to make the transition from practice room to barroom or tournament stage dictates how successful a career in darts you will have.

Playing at home on your own dartboard with friends is fine, but it may lack the element of real competition, so determine as soon as you can where darts is played in your area and join a club or league.

PREPARATION

If you are a casual player who merely walks into the bar hoping for a game, you might not be concerned about preparation, but for any competitive match, it is imperative.

Establish a routine where you check your darts, flights, and shafts and make sure you have spare darts and accessories readily available. If you are going to an arranged match, know the particulars: where the venue is, how you plan to get there (bus, train, car, cab, on foot), what time you have to be there, and the like. Give yourself a pep talk about the match, go over it in your mind, and make sure that you are mentally prepared for the challenge.

Practice at home before you leave and practice again at the venue. As long as you have done all you can (and perhaps a bit more) to prepare yourself for the game, you will be in the best position to do your best. This does not guarantee that you will win on any given night, but it will go a long way toward helping you achieve that goal.

PROFICIENCY

If your practice regime is working, then you will become a proficient darts player. Proficiency translates into concentration and confidence. It basically means that every time you step up to the throw line you are able to throw your darts accurately and precisely in an unhurried fashion and without fear of distraction. Thus, you are capable of winning matches regardless of what external circumstances—noise, gamesmanship, and the like—prevail. It is just you, your darts, and the dartboard. Nothing else matters.

Concentration

Whenever and wherever you play darts, there are bound to be distractions and therefore the ability to concentrate on the job at hand is vital for all darts players. You might well be a top player during your practice sessions in comfortable and familiar surroundings, but you must maintain your high standards in real-world competition.

There's an old darts adage: "Lose yourself in the match, but do not lose the match." Be sure that you are concentrating on your performance each time you step up to the throw line. Block out all distractions—verbal and visual—and focus on your game. Then, if a dart bounces off the dartboard or someone in the background shouts at you during your throw, you won't be thrown.

Confidence

You will win if you have the skills and confidence in those skills. Don't be your own worst enemy. For example, when you see who you are playing against, don't say to yourself, "Oh no. Not *him*." Who is he? He is actually the person who has to beat *you* in the game. You are ready and focused.

How often have you seen a player who misses an intended shot mouth the words "Come on!" to himself? To an opponent, that's the sign of a beaten man. After a disappointing shot, do not drop your head down, look depressed, or indulge in self-criticism. Having a talk with your darts will not help either. Do not send out any external signals of distress or disappointment. Your opponent will pick up on them and, as a result, his confidence level will go up.

When the darts do not all fly true, remain unmoved, remain confident. Fix the problem on the next throw. Concentrate on doing just that. Even if you lose the game, the match may not be lost. Concentrate on recovering in the next game. While a game or match is still winnable, never give up.

NERVES

Nerves can manifest themselves in many physical and mental forms.

All of a sudden, players may doubt their skills. They convince themselves that they are not good enough and that there is no way they can win. They feel physically sick or fidget with their darts. Their hands shake and they need to go to the bathroom (again) seconds before they are due to play. When they eventually toe the throw line, their practice darts go awry. The situation is dire before a competitive dart is thrown. There stands a beaten player.

Put simply, if you suffer from extreme nerves, you will never achieve a reasonable level of proficiency in darts. It is important to recognize that the problem exists and that it needs addressing. Then you can deal with the problem in the way best suited to you as an individual.

Dealing with extreme nerves is *not* about having a few drinks before each match. It is *not* about seeking out some magical medication. It is about coming to terms with the difficulties and addressing them in the appropriate way. It is about having faith in yourself and your skills. It is about achieving the correct mind-set to enable you to step up to any throw line in a confident manner, clearly knowing what needs to be done.

Some may need the services of a sports therapist, while others might solve their problems with the aid of self-help CDs. But usually the solution lies in being relaxed in mind and body—and focused.

TEMPERAMENT

All the hours spent at the practice dartboard count for nothing if you have the wrong temperament. If you are prone to anger, it must be controlled. If not, then anger will always be a potent threat to your success and your reputation as a darts player.

The majority of darts players will laugh off the occasional "bounce out" or the irony of ending up (yet again) on double 1. In a friendly game, most players will tolerate noise and chatter while they are throwing.

However, some will moan, curse, and throw down their darts—childish behavior in anyone's book.

While anger is a way of venting your emotions, it is of no benefit to your game whatsoever. Your opponent will stand by passively while you rant and rave. He—and everyone else—can see that you are losing it. Who do you think is the favorite to win the game now?

You are the only one who can control your emotions. Think about your behavior and, if necessary, remedy the situation as soon as you possibly can. Remember to treat your opponent the way you yourself wish to be treated.

RITUALS

Rituals and superstition are as common among darts players as they are among other sportsmen. Some darters will carry a lucky charm, use a set of lucky flights, or wear the same underwear every time they play a match.

It's easy for rituals and talismans to become a routine part of your preparation. But what happens if you misplace your lucky charm or you forget to pack your lucky blue bikini briefs? You may end up fixing your mind on the failed ritual and the perceived consequences rather than the game itself. You are defeated before you even toe the throw line. The best solution is not to have a ritual to begin with.

So, if you are starting out with darts, trash any ideas of clinging to a lucky charm—or lucky underwear for that matter. Rituals are very difficult to break once they are established.

DEDICATION

To become a top-class amateur or a professional player, there's no substitute for dedication.

Dedication separates the casual darter from the serious player. While a casual darts player may be content to play regularly, he is not necessarily dedicated to the game. To be dedicated means that you should be prepared to play darts any time, any place, anywhere and to schedule your work, your family, your leisure, indeed your entire life, around darts—not vice versa. Only by being dedicated—by being totally and exclusively focused on darts from dawn to dusk and beyond (yes, some players even *dream* darts)—can you ever expect to achieve greatness in the sport.

The dedicated darter will always carry his darts with him wherever he goes (except, of course, as carry-on luggage on aircraft!). You never know when an opportunity to play a game might arise.

A distilled version of dedication—enthusiasm—suffices for the majority of casual players. If that is what you want, then fair enough. But just accept that enthusiasm alone will not make you a *great* darts player.

PERSONAL FITNESS AND HEALTH

For the casual darts player, physical fitness may not be a priority when it comes to playing darts. Indeed, darts is still closely associated with bars where the emphasis is on drinking, socializing, and playing the game. For a long time, the archetypal image of a darts player was a fat, beer-swilling male (or sometimes female) who spent most of his evenings drinking and playing darts and then, at the end of a tiring evening, going out for a late-night meal. While that image is far from eradicated, there are signs of change.

The modern game of darts at the highest level now demands that players be fit. Once a player reaches major competition level, the formats of the games become longer. Such tournaments are a real test of stamina. A player could be on his feet for several hours. It is at times like these that players who have made the effort appreciate the benefits and reap the rewards of keeping fit.

THE FORMAL RULES

Finally, for the first time, I mention the *formality* of the sport. All national sports are played according to a set of rules, and they must be adhered to. Although these rules may change slightly from darts organization to darts organization, it is important for players to know the rules in whatever tournament or league match they play in. As an example, official Tournament Rules of the American Darts Organization are included in Appendix E.

I n all sports there are dangers and hazards to be overcome, some hidden and some blatantly obvious. Darts is no exception.

DARTS SAFETY

Undoubtedly, darts can be dangerous. They are sharp objects and should be respected as such. Darts is an adult sport. Be aware of this fact at all times. All responsible darts manufacturers make this clear with warnings printed on the packaging of their products such as: "This is a set of professional darts and is not a toy. Children should be supervised by an adult during play." Even soft-tip darts are potentially dangerous in the hands of children, so the same warnings apply.

In the standard game of darts, the main danger is from darts rebounding off the dartboard and hitting either one of the players, the scorer, or someone standing or sitting nearby. In most venues where major competitions are held, there's no one in the playing area apart from the players and officials, but at small bars and clubs, this is not always the case. People crowd around the throwing area to watch the game in progress. In such situations, injuries can occur, though thankfully they are rare.

Darts usually bounce out because of damage to either the dartboard or a dart. Adhere to the care and maintenance routine described in chapter 1. Make sure your darts are sharp. Check the dartboard before play and ask for it to be replaced if the wire spider looks too damaged. If the damage is only around the "red bit" (the triple 20), ask for the board to be turned.

The other cause of bounce-outs is the angry player. Darts thrown at the dartboard in anger are always a danger. There's no direction to the throw. The dart could end up anywhere. Control that temper and do not put others at risk.

THE VICE SQUAD: ALCOHOL, SMOKING, EATING, AND DRUGS

Whether it is eating, drinking or smoking, if you want to become a good player the bottom line must be: "Moderation in everything."

ALCOHOL

The truth is that alcohol has always been part of the culture of darts. After all, darts was born in the English public house and there it stayed relatively undisturbed for decades. When darts reached and swamped British television in the late 1970s, men who had previously only tossed darts in their local pubs and clubs or annual contests such as the *News of the World* Individual Darts Championship were thrown into the spotlight—and their alcohol (and smoking) accompanied them on to what became a world stage. Every broadcast of a match showed the majority of players lifting a pint of beer or lager to their lips and having a puff on a cigarette between throws.

Nonetheless, quaffing vast amounts of alcohol will not make you a better darts player. Alcohol compromises your coordination and concentration—two essential ingredients for darts success. It makes you wonder how much better some of the darters of yesteryear would have played had they not drunk fifteen pints of Guinness before a match!

If you enjoy a drink, drink in moderation. Celebrate a victory or drown your sorrows after a defeat with a drink, but do not do so to excess. Your darts will fly all the better for your restraint.

Smoking

Smoking has recently become an absolute no-no in the United States, the UK, and parts of Europe. Where a ban is in effect, this includes no smoking in public places, which naturally includes pubs, bars, sports arenas, and even private clubs. Even before formal statutory smoking bans were introduced, as with alcohol, those in charge of the sport had banned smoking from the stages of major darts events. For many years, across the world, tobacco companies sponsored darts competitions, but this, too, ceased in European countries in the year 2000.

Eating

If you want to achieve in any sport, diet is vitally important. All that is needed here is for all darts players to be reminded that overindulging in food can affect your game as much as smoking or drinking to excess. Your gastronomic activities offstage can and will affect your performance on the throw line. Too much eating makes you lazy and that laziness will, undoubtedly, affect your game. Darts is about concentration, so whether it is simply that the food has made you uncomfortable, has given you wind, or it is making you think, "I've eaten too much," all are distractions—and sometimes quite painful and embarrassing ones—to the game at hand. If you are concerned about your diet or your weight, consider discussing the issue with your doctor.

Drugs

All organized sports worldwide acknowledge that the use of performance-enhancing drugs is a major problem. It has only been in recent years that darts organizations have set about addressing such abuse in major competitions. Random drug testing of professional darts players was introduced into the UK by both the British Darts Organisation (BDO) and the Darts Regulation Authority (DRA) although, strangely enough, the definition of *drugs* does not include alcohol.

GAMESMANSHIP

Gamesmanship is defined as "skill in using ploys to gain a victory or advantage over another person."

The English author Stephen Potter wrote a book about gamesmanship in the 1940s and subtitled his work *The Art of Winning Games without Actually Cheating.* Applying this "art" to darts, Potter recommended that a player "Question your darts opponent closely on the exact area of the dart where he deems it wisest to exert maximum thumb-and-finger pressure. Continue to ask if he will be so kind as to demonstrate for you the precise position of the hand in relation to the head and the moment when the dart is released . . ." Hardly the act of a sportsman!

Sadly, the possibilities for gamesmanship are endless. As you try to throw, your opponent may click his darts while standing behind you, shuffle his feet, clink glasses together, talk to you, play with the change or keys in his pocket, "accidentally" drop his darts, or make "natural sounds" (such as clearing the throat, coughing, or whistling). Blowing smoke in an opponent's eyes used to be another tactic, but this has now been eradicated with the smoking ban in public places.

One of the most common forms of gamesmanship involves a player deliberately slowing down the speed of the game, either by throwing his own darts slowly or by taking his time in removing his darts from the dartboard after his turn—or both. This can destroy another player's rhythm and concentration, which is, of course, the whole point of the strategy. Rest assured, though, that darts players cannot maintain a long winning streak by using these methods. Also, if you are in a league, officials will eventually take disciplinary action against the offenders.

Keep this in mind: In the majority of friendly games, anything goes. Gamesmanship is seen as part of the fun of playing casual darts. It is, therefore, to be expected, and each player has the opportunity to give as good as he gets. Playing darts for fun allows the rules of common courtesy to be broken by mutual agreement.

THE CROWD

Over and above the opposition, you may have a crowd with which to contend.

At all darts venues, large or small, there will be people watching and supporting their team or their favorite player. Calling out while a player is throwing or heckling him during the game is very common. While this is frowned upon, it is impossible for the referee or other officials to control the behavior of the crowd (or isolated elements of it) 100 percent of the time. It is up to the individual players to prepare themselves psychologically for such interruptions.

You can concentrate and train yourself to block out any noise, but the sounds of the crowd can be unpredictable. One solution is to record a CD or load your MP3 player full of occasional and irregular interruptions and to play it when practicing at home. Start the CD from a different position each time so that you do not become used to the rhythm of the interruptions.

STAYING COOL

Good darts players at any level prepare themselves psychologically for each game, and over time gain experience in how to deal with gamesmanship, crowd noise, or any other type of distraction.

Be aware of each and every trick, and teach yourself to ignore them all. Ignore any sly comment from your opponent, such as a compliment on a good first dart that is clearly intended as a distraction. Do not reply. Concentrate on the game at hand. Maintain your focus and play on.

If your opponent suddenly needs to fit a new shaft onto a dart or requests a bathroom break, cope with such interruptions in an agreeable and carefree manner. Relax and stay focused on your game. In a tournament setting, there may be established official rules that forbid such interruptions, so make sure you're aware of them.

If an opponent does try to slow the game down or speed it up, calmly await your next turn. Do not try to adjust your speed to compensate. You know the rhythm of your game, so maintain it, no matter how long you may have to wait for your next turn. If you let any tension seep into your game, then it may well be lost.

Another mental pitfall to avoid: Don't be in a hurry to finish off your opponent. Players often tighten up when victory is within reach. Maintain your nerve and your rhythm. Think of that winning double as any other target. You have practiced long and hard for this moment. Enjoy it.

Finally, try not to psych yourself out when you're playing an opponent you know is superior. Give it your best. It is surprising how, in such circumstances, you often raise the level of your game. You may not win, but you may do much better than you anticipated. Remember that top players can have off days. Of course, to beat the very best on one of his bad days, you might need to have one of your very best days.

DARTITIS

The word *dartitis* was first coined in the UK in 1981 by Tony Wood, the then-editor of *Darts World* magazine, to describe a condition whereby a darts player finds himself in the position of being unable to release his darts, a condition often compared with the "yips" in golf. Players who had played darts for years (including five-time World Champion Eric Bristow) suddenly discovered that they had dartitis.

In 2007, the word appeared for the first time in the Oxford English Dictionary. It is defined as "a state of nervousness which prevents a player from releasing a dart at the right moment when throwing."

Despite a significant amount of research into the sources of and remedies for this condition, there's no single solution to the problem of dartitis.

Most research confirms that it is a psychological condition, but opinions differ on the causes and the treatments. For example, one left-handed player overcame his dartitis by learning to throw his darts right-handed. Others have changed their darts for lighter or heavier ones or revised their stance and throw. Such was the concern that grew up around dartitis in the 1980s that an urban myth was established that standing in a bucket of water would drive the affliction away!

In the late 1980s, I was struck with the condition, but eventually banished my dartitis by changing both my style of play and my psychological approach to the game. I wrote at the time, "I threw more slowly, taking a deep breath before the throw and expelling it *with* the throw. I also concentrated more on the dartboard and tried to block out all external noise. It was just me against the board. I also stopped drinking strong cider, switching back to good old real ale." Another player suffering from the condition cured it by taking up weight lifting. His arms became strong and firm. His confidence grew and the problem simply went away. In 1987, Eric Bristow treated his dartitis by reverting to a style of throw he had used pre-1983, changing his diet by cutting out junk food, and curbing his drinking.

With so many suggested "cures," the somewhat unsatisfying answer is that each individual must find his own solution. However, a return to fundamentals is always a wise first step in dealing with dartitis. And one can always hope that the affliction never strikes!

The history of the sport of darts has traditionally been "lost in the mists of alehouse smoke." Though customary accounts would tell you otherwise, the game of darts that we all know and enjoy today is *not* centuries old. The truth is that modern darts is less than one hundred years old.

Very few authors have spent time examining the history of darts. Those who tried to illuminate darts' past tended to repeat and recycle fragments that had been published in previous works; some even gilded earlier stories with additional information that, until they had picked up their pens, had never previously existed. The power of the imagination (and lazy research) managed to totally distort what little was known about the origins of the sport.

DARTS: THE EARLY YEARS

According to the Oxford English Dictionary (OED), the word *dart* originally meant "a light, throwing-spear which did not necessarily have stabilizing vanes" and darts or "light javelins" are traced back to the late Stone Age. The OED's earliest reference to "dartes" is circa 1314. However, *darts* defined as a form of recreation does not find its way in the OED until well into the twentieth century.

In 1801, Joseph Strutt published his major work, *Sports and Pastimes of the People of England.* The book focused on both rural and domestic recreations from the earliest times to the then-present day. He described games in which darts were blown rather than thrown. These games, known as "puff and dart," "puff the dart," or "puff darts," were in fact the forerunners of the modern game of darts. The game consisted of blowing small darts through a tube at a concentric, miniature archery target; the contestant who earned the highest score with three puffed darts was declared the winner.

By the nineteenth century, puff and dart was well-established in pubs in major towns and cities throughout England. The game later found its way into the homes of wealthy Victorians as it gained popularity as "drawing room archery." In 1883, the dangers of playing puff and dart were highlighted in the British medical journal, *The Lancet*. Due to the frequency of people drawing the small darts down into their stomachs or lungs (sucking at the blowpipe instead of blowing), doctors condemned the practice as highly dangerous. Fortunately, it was about this time that larger, hand-propelled wooden darts were imported from France and built on the existing popularity of puff and darts.

Though darts has always been viewed as the most traditional of English pub games, the origins of the modern game lie principally in the importation of wooden "French darts." For many years, an early form of darts, known as *javelot* or *flechettes,* had been played in French cafés and bars. This game attracted the attention of British showmen who introduced French darts into their fairground sideshows but used targets of their own design.

Brian Gamlin, the man credited with devising the ingenious (and devious) numbering system of the modern dartboard, might well have been a showman. The fact that no record of the man can be traced could indicate that he was always on the move. Remember that showmen were (and are) always looking to increase the odds in their favor, so the introduction of a numbered board rather than a concentric, miniature archery target would have made it more difficult for a customer to win a prize. Traveling the length and breadth of England, the showmen introduced the new game of darts in hundreds of communities, which led slowly but surely to darts being introduced into pubs.

THE GAME CATCHES ON

Darts was making some progress—progress that appeared to have been halted when a Leeds pub owner was brought before the local magistrates in what became known as the "Annakin case." In 1908, James Garside, landlord of the Adelphi Inn, was summoned to appear before Leeds magistrates on the charge of allowing a game of chance, namely darts, to be played in his establishment. To aid his case, Garside called on his top champion of the game, William "Big Foot" Annakin. After a demonstration of darts to the court by Annakin, the judgment was that darts was a game of skill and not a game of chance. Darts was therefore legal and the case was dismissed, although any game, including darts, played for money continued to be illegal.

After the turn of the twentieth century, modern darts became increasingly popular and was set to expand beyond anyone's imagination. For many years the brewery trade had been under pressure from governments, temperance movements, and religious organizations to improve the nature of their business or, as some would have preferred, to close their pubs altogether. Debate came to a head in the late nineteenth and early twentieth century and some brewers decided to improve their premises. Mostly, this meant tearing down old beerhouses and pubs with bad reputations and replacing them with respectable, well-lit, and more welcoming premises. The "improvements" included the introduction or re-promotion of new or existing pub games.

The first three decades of the twentieth century saw the further development of previously existing leisure pursuits and the arrival of new alternative entertainments, especially from the United States. These included movies, dance halls, and greyhound racing, which, by the mid- to late

1920s, would all be competing for the small amounts of disposable income the working-class pubgoer had in his pocket. Thus, the brewers introduced (or in some cases, re-promoted) darts into their pubs, promoting the game as a counterattraction to the developing threats to the English pub.

Darts was played by servicemen and women "behind the lines" during World War I in the recreation huts provided by the YMCA. Such games as darts and dominoes were small, portable, took up little space, and were ideally suited to the conditions of war. Darts came to the attention of many soldiers unfamiliar with the game, which helped fire the expansion of darts in Britain and elsewhere after the conflict ended.

The interwar period witnessed an explosion of games in English pubs, the most popular being darts, shove ha'penny, rings (also known as "indoor quoits"), dominoes, cribbage, and skittles. In 1925, the *Brewers' Journal* reported that "in licensed premises throughout the country no factor stands out with more prominence than the facilities existing for the pursuit of indoor recreations," adding that "the provision of indoor games was distinctly an exception prior to 1914." This explains why it has been so difficult to trace the prehistory of darts and other now well-established pub games.

In 1924, representatives of the brewing industry, the licensed trade, and members of darts leagues met in London to work out ways of further promoting darts. It had been clear since 1918 that the game was generating much interest and enthusiasm, and the number of leagues was increasing day by day. However, the way the game was played and the targets used differed from one place to the next. These men meeting in London set about the task of standardizing the game.

The result was the formation in 1925 of the National Darts Association (NDA). The purpose of the NDA was to introduce and promote a standard set of rules for the game, to protect the game from "fanatics" (those who would use the game for illegal gambling purposes), and to make darts "a pure, clean, and skilful [sic] sport worthy to rank with any other." The impact on the development of darts was immediate, especially in London and the southeast area of England, and soon hundreds of darts leagues were set up.

The "London" game, with its dartboard that included a triple ring (counting three times the value of the segment) and an outer bull's-eye ring, wasn't readily accepted in the north of the country, where they had their own regional dartboards, including the Yorkshire board and the smaller Manchester log-end board. Indeed, these areas did not accept the London board until the 1970s, when the second boom in the sport took place and, even today, there remain pockets of resistance.

THE FIRST BOOM

The first darts boom occurred during the mid- to late 1930s in England, centering on the capital. In 1927, the popular Sunday newspaper the *News of the World* joined forces with the NDA to run an individual darts competition for darts players in the metropolitan area of London. It was described as a "darts test" to identify the best darts player. More than a thousand players entered and the winner was Sammy Stone, a Boer War veteran, father of nine, and slater (roofer) by trade. Such was the popularity of the *News of the World* competition that by 1938 it encompassed most of England and Wales and the total number of entrants for the 1938–1939 season exceeded 250,000. It was the darts contest every working man (and occasionally woman) wanted to win. It was one of the few chances the common man had of becoming a champion.

The interest generated by the *News of the World,* the growing number of brewery leagues, and the promotional prowess of the NDA brought darts to the attention of the middle and upper classes in England in the latter part of the 1930s. Newspaper reports indicated that darts had become "the pastime of kings, cabinet ministers, novelists, stage, screen, and sports stars." When King George VI and Queen Elizabeth threw a few darts at a community center in Slough, Berkshire, in December 1937, the country went "darts mad" and women inundated the offices of the NDA for instructions on how to play the "Royal Game." Darts champions appeared in cabarets in London and other large towns and cities, and were featured as demonstrators of the game in sports departments of major stores. Darts saloons were established in London, where the middle and upper classes could go to learn the game.

The elite's infatuation with darts was short-lived and, with the coming of war, the darts saloons closed. Many leagues, finding membership depleted by war service, were suspended. However, darts was to play a major role in boosting morale, both in Britain and abroad, between 1939 and 1945. The game of darts was played by British servicemen and servicewomen across all theaters of war and was even played in Prisoner of War camps, including, perhaps surprisingly, some in Japan and Burma.

Servicemen and -women from other countries, such as the United States and Canada, who were stationed in Britain during the war, found themselves (and their money) welcomed in pubs up and down the country. For many of them, this was their first exposure to English beer and English pub games. World War II was responsible in large part for spreading the game of darts across the globe, although it would be some time before the game properly established itself in other countries.

After 1945, darts in Britain returned to being a working-class pub game. The NDA did not survive the war. Even though hundreds of thousands of darts players continued to enter the *News of the World* Individual Darts Championship, darts remained a low-profile pastime and had little or no status as a sport.

THE SECOND BOOM—AND BEYOND

In the early 1970s, Olly Croft, an avid London darts player, darts organizer, and the owner of a tile company, saw the potential of darts as a televised sport. He set about transforming a mere pub game into a national—and, eventually, an international—sport. Croft gathered around him some other darts enthusiasts who eventually formed the British Darts Organisation (BDO). Under the BDO's auspices, darts swamped British television, and sponsors were falling all over themselves to become involved with the game.

Although darts had been televised in Britain occasionally since 1939, viewers had seen nothing like the deluge of darts during the late 1970s to the mid-1980s. As the number of viewers increased to unprecendented levels, the first darts "superstars" appeared, such as Wales' Leighton Rees, England's Eric Bristow and John Lowe, and Scotland's Jocky Wilson. This exposure and success led to much interest in the game from other countries, particularly the United States. In a stroke of genius, Croft led the establishment of the World Darts Federation (WDF), which sought to link all the darts organizations across the globe and to encourage other emergent darts-playing countries to set up their own national organizations. Today there are over sixty member countries of the WDF.

However, TV executives decided to change the image of their broadcasts in the mid-1980s, and darts was one of the first sports to suffer as a result. Telecasts of darts contests had been slowing gradually, but when the TV executives all at once spurned darts completely (except for the Embassy World Championship), the sport was thrown into turmoil.

By the early 1990s, professional darts players were increasingly unhappy with the situation and believed that little more could be achieved by the BDO. Sixteen "rebel" players, including top stars like Bristow and Lowe, joined forces with their managers and members of the darts industry and entrusted their future to a new darts organization, the World Darts Council (WDC)—later to become the Professional Darts Corporation (PDC). This sent the darts world into free fall, with the BDO and WDC making claims and counterclaims against each other. In 1997, the WDC won a court action over restraint of trade, and some of the pressure eased, but the exchange of views (to put it mildly) continues to this day.

The WDC (now the PDC) succeeded in attracting satellite TV coverage, and over recent years the number of annually televised events through that medium has increased substantially. Meanwhile, at the time of this writing, the BDO events broadcast on terrestrial British television number only two—the Lakeside (formerly the Embassy) World Professional Darts Championship and the WINMAU World Masters. The PDC has also made inroads in terrestrial TV with the introduction of the Grand Slam of Darts in November 2007. With the ongoing success of the PDC, there has been a mass migration of players to the PDC from the BDO ranks.

Many darts fans want to see the BDO and the PDC working together, but this is highly unlikely. The lines are now firmly drawn. The Professional Darts Corporation, as its title suggests, concentrates solely on showcasing professional darts players and has little or no interest in the grass roots of the game. The BDO continues to run youth, county, and national darts leagues and competitions and provides a quality breeding ground for the darting stars of the future, while the WDF organizes international darts under its auspices.

THE HISTORY OF DARTS IN THE UNITED STATES

Contrary to myth, the Pilgrims did not introduce darts to the New World. My research and that of American darts historian Dan William Peek reveal no record in the log of the Mayflower to suggest that they engaged in any frivolous activities, let alone darts.

The consensus of opinion is that darts entered the United States toward the end of the nineteenth century in the coal-mining region of Philadelphia and possibly New Jersey. In addition, Dan Peek, in his book *To the Point: The Story of Darts in America*, revealed that the first person to hang a dartboard on an American tavern wall was John Pearson, circa 1900.

Pearson owned a tavern at the corner of Ridge and Nicetown Lane in Philadelphia.

At the cutting edge of darts in Philadelphia between the world wars was the Widdy Manufacturing Company which, Peek discovered, introduced cork-faced, plywood-backed dartboards, featuring the English numbering sequence, in the 1930s. This timing corresponds very nicely with the first darts boom in England.

By the late 1950s, the English game had gathered some momentum in America. In 1959, the first "international" match between Britain and the United States was played in New York City. The venue was the Market Diner on Twelfth Avenue and the teams were composed of members of the crews of the *Queen Elizabeth* and the *United States*. To the absolute delight of the American team and their supporters, the English were defeated five games to four. However, in the return match played the following year, the Americans were routed four games to one.

American interest in the game continued to grow, albeit slowly, so that by the end of the 1960s organized darts leagues could be found not only in Philadelphia and New York but also in Atlanta, Boston, Cleveland, Dallas, Detroit, Los Angeles, San Diego, San Francisco, and many other cities and towns. Such was the popularity of the game that in 1969 the United States Darting Association (USDA) was established.

In 1973, America sent its first representative to play in the prestigious *News of the World* Individual Darts Championship at the Alexandra Palace in London. The thirty-eight-year-old pub owner, Philadelphia's Al "The Iceman" Lippman, was undaunted by the prospect of playing darts against the best, but suffered a 2–0 first-round defeat to then-champion of Wales, Tony Ridler.

In 1974, a select USDA team took on a team of the best players Britain could offer and trounced the Brits 9–6. Played at the Royal Manhattan Hotel in New York, the match left the British team—and the darts world in general—in shock for many months. To add insult to injury, during that same year, George Silberzahn, a darts shooter from Gibbstown, Pennsylvania, ran through a field that included sixty-one of the best players Britain could offer to win the USDA's inaugural Open International Classic.

With the advent of the British Darts Organisation in England in the mid-1970s, the long reach of Olly Croft brought American darts under the umbrella organization, the World Darts Federation. Pivotal to the organization of darts in the United States from that time was the American Darts Organization (ADO).

The rise in popularity of traditional darts over recent years in Britain has not been mirrored in the United States. One of the reasons for this is the increased American interest in "soft-tip" or electronic darts.

A BRIEF HISTORY OF ELECTRONIC ("SOFT-TIP") DARTS

Over the past thirty years, electronic or "soft-tip" darts (so named because the points of the darts are made of plastic rather than steel) has gained a considerable toehold in the United States, Japan, and some European countries. The idea of a dartboard constructed in such a way that pressure pads (or other technology) behind the segments electronically register the score as each dart strikes is not new. As early as 1934, Maurice Elliott and Baden Warne, both of Suffolk, England, filed a patent for an application "relating to apparatus for playing games or for instructional purposes," which related to "a scoreboard or target, divided into a plurality of scoring areas and comprising electrodes adapted to be bridged by a dart or other projectile piercing a scoring area to complete a circuit through a corresponding electrically operated score indicator, and separated by a sheet of insulating material formed as a unit applicable to or removable from the board as a single entity."

The invention was shown applied to a standard dartboard.

The principle—registering the score by electronic means—has remained the same over the years, but, of course, the technology has vastly improved.

The soft-tip revolution in the United States began in the 1980s with electronic dart games produced by Arachnid Inc. (a company named after the spider because the wiring of the dartboard resembles a spider's web).

As Timothy R. Bucci, author of *A Quiver of 3: Soft-Tip Darts for the New Player*, states, soft-tip darts have today become "an integral part of the amusement industry" in the United States. According to *Play Meter* magazine, in 2004 the estimated annual income generated by electronic darts machines in the United States was $131 million.

In Japan, where technology is embraced with fervor and where only a couple of major cities have venues for traditional darts, the soft-tip version is played by many thousands of enthusiasts.

Since the early 1990s, a good number of attempts have been made to launch and promote the soft-tip game in the UK, and all have failed miserably. The British can be stubborn and are known to hang on to their heritage for dear life, and so it is with darts. The general view is that "We invented darts," so the British will resist the electronic game not only for nostalgic reasons but also because "We do not like other people (especially the Americans) messing about with our games." ("See what they did to the very English game of rounders?") The other reason is that games in British pubs have always—with a small number of exceptions, such as bar billiards and pool—been free to play. Paying for a game of darts is anathema to English pubgoers, and so far all attempts to engage them with electronic darts have proved pointless.

However, if anyone thinks that soft-tip will never invade the UK, they should think again. It *will* eventually come and gradually edge out the traditional game. It will not happen today or even next year, but in this electronic, computerized age, where young people are continually in search of new amusements, it *will* happen.

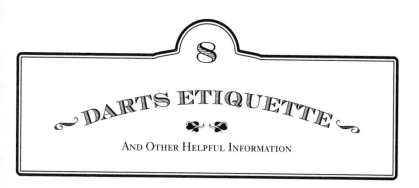

~ DARTS ETIQUETTE ~

AND OTHER HELPFUL INFORMATION

The first section of this chapter will deal with the etiquette of the sport and the common courtesy that should be extended to all players. We then move on to look at the referee and the range of darts venues.

DARTS ETIQUETTE

Darts etiquette is a combination of written and unwritten rules, tradition, and common courtesy—the "manners" of darts play.

In any sport, there should be respect for your opponents, whether you particularly care for them or not.

Always begin any darts match with a handshake and, if you like, wish your opponent good luck. While your opponent is at the line, throwing his three darts, stand silently and motionless behind him, and do not engage in any form of gamesmanship (see chapter 6).

After your turn, do not walk back toward your opponent. After you have taken your darts out of the dartboard, walk up the side of the throwing area and take your position behind the player. Why? Heading back toward him may break his concentration and rhythm and lead to accusations of gamesmanship. Plus, he may well be a fast thrower and have begun releasing his first dart!

Conversation or making comments during a game is completely out of the question. Both players must be allowed to concentrate on their game to the exclusion of everything else. Even complimentary remarks, such as "good darts" or "nice shot," during a turn could be construed as interference. If an audience is present, players must desist from directing remarks to them as well.

Whether you win or lose, when a match is over, turn to your opponent and shake his hand. If you have lost the match, congratulate him on his win. In British pub and club matches, it was traditional for the loser to offer to buy the winner a drink. However, although a nice gesture, it is not as common or expected today as it used to be.

If you lose, do not make excuses for your poor performance that might belittle your opponent's success or make you out to be a poor loser. Phrases like, "My tennis elbow has been acting up a bit this week," "That's what I get for not practicing enough," or "You caught me on a bad day" are inappropriate and uncalled for.

Another tradition within pubs and clubs is for players to indicate that they wish to play by chalking their names on the scoreboard and then scoring the next game. For many years, darts was scored with chalk on a blackboard; thus, to score a game was known as "taking the chalks." When chalking a game, the chalker must not look at the players throwing their darts. Not only is this distracting for the darters, but it is clear that the scorer is not paying attention to what is being scored on the dartboard. Out of respect for the other players, concentrate on the dartboard and announce the scores clearly after each throw of three darts.

Then there's the crowd. Crowd control at any darts match is difficult, but common courtesy requires fans to remain quiet while each player takes a turn. They can then make as much noise as they like between throws. In the early days of organized darts, this was achieved effectively as respect for each player was greeted with silence as they played, followed by shouting after the throw, followed again by absolute quiet as the next player toed the throw line. Recently, however, tournaments have attracted larger and rowdier crowds. The big events have become very much like trying to play darts in your local pub or club.

THE DARTS REFEREE

In most informal games of darts at home, in the pub or bar, or elsewhere, a referee is not required. However, in all top tournaments a referee is essential to ensure that the rules and etiquette of the game are strictly adhered to. The referee also has to keep an eye on the chalkers (those marking the score sheets) so that he can be certain that the score sheets accurately reflect the players' scores and that any corrections are made so as not to disturb the players' throws.

The referee should have all the rules at his fingertips so he is able to settle any dispute as quickly as possible. He must also be quick at mental arithmetic. In addition to being able to accurately call the scores, the referee must be able to answer questions such as "What does that leave me?" Players must have confidence in the referee's ability to answer their questions promptly and decisively so they themselves can make a quick decision as to where they should throw their next dart. A good referee must also have a commanding voice, a no-nonsense attitude when it comes to crowd control, and a sharp eye for gamesmanship among the players. In short, the referee is *the* authority during a match.

WHERE TO PLAY

Darts is an extremely adaptable game. It can literally be played anywhere, even in space. In 1973 and 1974, specially made darts and a dartboard were taken aboard Skylab as part of the official Off Duty Activities Equipment (ODAE). According to NASA, the game was taken "purely as a form of entertainment and not for any type of research." This brought a whole new meaning to the term "away game."

Back on earth, darts can be played both outdoors and indoors. However, few serious games are played outside. In the 1970s, one or two competitions were held in the open in the UK, but fell foul of the weather. Outdoor darts is generally played for pure recreational fun with family and friends.

Pubs, bars, and clubs are by far the most obvious locations for a dartboard. Provided you are of an age that allows you to enter such premises, seek out the best place. A number of bars might provide a dartboard, but check out which owner takes a more serious interest in the sport.

Undertake some research and spend some time talking to bar owners to find the place that is right for you. One of the biggest giveaways of a darts-oriented pub is, of course, the number of dartboards hanging on the walls. The sight of numerous electronic darts machines will immediately indicate that the place is a center for soft-tip play.

If you experience a severe attack of darts fever, you will likely seek out serious league play, which will often involve joining a team. If you hope to become a top-notch player, there's no point in joining a team of friendly players who only play for booze and laughs.

To elevate your game, you'll need to constantly challenge yourself. You may eventually outgrow your first darts team, in which case you should look to transfer your skills to a better team, preferably one in a higher league. You may even find yourself being headhunted by another team. Many good darts players become comfortable with a team and never progress beyond it—and such contentment may cause them to fail to reach their true potential.

Over and above the normal pub and club darts teams in the UK, there is a formal structure for progression that is mainly played under the control and the rules of the British Darts Organisation (BDO).

For more information on becoming involved in organized darts in the United States, visit the American Darts Organization's Web site (www.adodarts.com).

9

WOMEN'S DARTS

With its roots in the male-oriented English pub, darts has taken some time to be adopted by women. Nevertheless, women are playing quality darts nowadays and some top ladies are a match for the fellas. This chapter provides a short history of women's darts and then looks closely at the women's game.

A BRIEF HISTORY OF WOMEN'S DARTS

Until World War II was over, women and girls in the UK were afforded few opportunities to play either casually or competitively. Few ever ventured out to the pub unless on a weekend accompanied by a husband or boyfriend. The public bar was traditionally regarded as a male preserve. However, as the 1930s progressed, English brewers continued to improve their pubs and provide facilities for women. More and more women went into pubs on a regular basis and were exposed to darts.

By the mid-1930s, many brewers (always looking for additional ways to make money) experimented with separate women's darts leagues—and they became extremely popular. It was a great way for women to be allowed into pubs—in groups rather than as individuals—and thus the stigma of a single woman in a pub began to fade. Some ambitious women even entered the *News of the World* individual darts competition, and a small number made it through to the Area or Divisional Finals. However, these were isolated cases.

Ladies darts leagues were one thing, but allowing women to play on a men's team was another matter entirely. In 1937, for example, in the South Shields and District Darts League, two teams had "ten women between them." Such was the furor at this discovery that an emergency meeting (all male) was held and the decision reached that "mixed darts must cease" and the women were thrown out.

In December 1937, King George VI and Queen Elizabeth visited a new community center in Slough, Berkshire, and played a brief game of darts (only three darts each) that the Queen won. It sent the whole nation—especially the women—into a darts frenzy. Shortly after the "Royal Darts Match," a Sunday newspaper headline read: "Women Flock to Follow the Queen's Lead at Darts."

However, it was not until the mid-1970s that women's darts would be taken seriously, and even then, despite the herculean efforts of the British Darts Organisation (BDO), it never attracted the all-important sponsorship or television coverage. Regrettably, except for the WINMAU Women's World Masters and the Lakeside Women's World Professional Darts Championship, this remains the case to this day and TV coverage of women's darts remains scant. Thus very few women are able to make a living from the sport

For many years, women darts players either failed to qualify, or were not allowed to enter, the preliminary rounds of major competitions. However, in 2000, Gayl King, Canada's number one women's player and the number seven–ranked women's player in the world, was written into the history books when she received a wild card to enter the Professional Darts Corporation's World Championship at the Circus Tavern, Purfleet, Essex, England. Although she lost the match against the world-ranked number thirty-two player, Graeme Stoddart, she did win a set against him. While King told reporters "This was my dream and I lived it," Stoddart dismissed the whole matter, saying that inviting King to take part had been a good publicity stunt.

Publicity stunt or not, her invitation to play in the PDC championship against the men seemed to galvanize the BDO into action. The following year, the BDO introduced the first-ever Women's World Darts Championship. Today this remains the top prize in women's darts. The inaugural winner was England's Trina Gulliver, who successfully defended her title for six successive years, eventually regaining her world title in 2010.

WOMEN AND DARTS

In May 1978, the Embassy World Professional Darts Champion, Welsh darts star Leighton Rees, said, "I think we'll soon see the time when the world men's champion will lose to a woman. There are some great girl players on the circuit now . . . ." More than thirty years later and only three players, England's Trina Gulliver, Holland's Francis Hoenselaar, and Russia's Anastasia Dobromyslova, come anywhere near, on a regular basis, to achieving averages that would threaten the best male darters.

Why should this be?

Though the standard image of a darts player is always male—and often not a flattering image at that—over the years, darts has become a women's game, too. There is certainly no reason why women cannot compete at the same level as men. Darts is not a sport reliant on power and physical strength; the skills required are equally suited to both women and men.

Of course, there's no difference in the target to be aimed at or in the distance of the throw line. It seems the problem comes when a player wants to become more than a casual darter. For married women—especially those with children—family responsibilities reduce the opportunities to play competitively and practice. Even if we like to fancy that we live in an enlightened age of equality, the truth is that this balancing act is not expected of male darters—at least not those who have achieved great success.

If you'll indulge some observations and armchair sociology, it does seem that at the bar level—where players often shape their "commitment" to darts—men and women tend to approach the game differently. For men, the darts competition with their pals is often the primary focus of their evening. For women, the darts—while enjoyable—are secondary to socializing. These are, of course, generalizations. There are plenty of women who delight in cutthroat competition at the dartboard and plenty of men who would rather toss back a few beers and have some laughs than toss their darts. But, still, the culture of pub darts tends to net more serious male players than female ones.

Nonetheless, being able to play darts has nothing whatsoever to do with gender. If a player—female or male—spends sufficient time practicing, is in good physical and mental condition, and is totally committed to the game, success will come.

According to Dr. Linda Duffy, a top academic in the field of sports psychology with particular reference to darts, regardless of gender and physical differences, superior darts performance is related to the "accumulated number of hours engaged in various types of deliberate practice." In other words: practice, practice, and more practice.

The age-old chauvinistic attitudes and sexism are gradually diminishing in the world of darts. Female players are starting to earn some respect. As Leighton Rees once said, "They're not women darts players; they're just darts players."

Women have their own Lakeside Women's Professional Darts Championship and WINMAU Women's World Masters events but, to date, other sponsors seem uninterested in backing them in any other major events, although in the UK one or two top female darters are invited to participated in the Grand Slam of Darts against the men. Thus very few women darts players are able to make a living from the sport.

10

TOURNAMENTS

A t some point in the lives of all serious darts players, their thoughts will turn to finding out how good they really are. The best way to do this is to enter tournaments. Nowhere else can such experience be gained. In local matches, the likelihood is that you will play against the same faces month after month and year after year. Only by broadening your horizons and entering competitive open tournaments can you really test yourself and your skills against the best.

If you want to play in tournaments, you need to know where to find information about up-and-coming competitions. Local darts contests may be advertised in local newspapers, league newsletters, or simply by word of mouth in a particular pub. All major darting organizations have Web sites that provide up-to-date information relating to competitions, rules, deadlines, and how to enter (and pay your fee) online. Large national darts tournaments are normally publicized through the darts press, such as *BEN (Bull's Eye News)* in the United States and *Darts World* and *We Love Darts* in the UK.

For all tournaments, potential players must check the rules of entry into the competition. First, make sure that you are entitled to play. Many competitions are closed to everyone except members of a certain club or organization. Once you are satisfied that you can apply, check the remaining details. Where is the venue? Can you get there easily? Will you have to make arrangements to stay somewhere overnight to ensure that you arrive in time for registration? When do you have to register? Do you have to pay the entry fee (or a part of it) upfront and, if so, how much and by when?

SOME KEY TOURNAMENTS PAST AND PRESENT

Things change so quickly in the world of darts that to mention a large number of current major tournaments here would be counterproductive, inasmuch as names, dates, sponsors, rules, and conditions are likely to change shortly after this book goes to press, if not before. Even those few cited here occasionally review and revise their formats (as was done in the WINMAU World Masters in 2007). This, then, is a personal selection of some of the most important darts competitions ever to be played on the planet; they are also the main tournament titles that darts players past and present have aspired to win.

The *News of the World* Individual Darts Championship

The *News of the World* Individual Darts Championship was the tournament that, for decades, all English working-class darts players wanted to win. The *News of the World* (the most popular Sunday newspaper in Britain) promoted the competition through its pages and gave the grand prize of a huge silver trophy to be kept by the winner's pub for a year. The winner himself received a replica cup and a medal. There was no cash prize until the late 1970s. The format was a simple one: the best of three games (most commonly called "legs").

It was the only sports title that the ordinary working man (or woman) had any chance of winning. The entry fee was small and all the preliminary rounds of the competition were played in local pubs. Just over one thousand entries were received for the inaugural contest in 1927–1928 but by the 1938–1939 season there were over 250,000 darts players vying for six divisional titles.

In 1978, the British Darts Organisation (BDO) ran its first Embassy (later Lakeside) World Professional Darts Championship (see below) and many saw this as direct competition to the *News of the World*—which, of course, it was. As the Embassy World Championship grew in popularity and was regularly featured on BBC television, the stature of the *News of the World* began to fade. In 1990, due to lack of sponsorship and a change in the editorial direction of the newspaper, the *News of the World* Individual Darts Championship was "suspended." It was revived for one season during 1996–1997 but was then suspended once more, never again to see the light of day. The *News of the World* continues to be one of the most popular Sunday newspapers in the UK and reports regularly on other top darts tournaments.

Although the *News of the World* Individual Darts Championship is no more, all darts players should be aware of the national and later worldwide importance of this competition in spreading the word about darts.

North American Open Darts Tournament

In the 1970s and 1980s, the North American Open Darts Tournament (NAODT) ranked among the most prestigious darts competitions in the United States, along with the Santa Monica Open and the Golden Gate Classic.

It was the brainchild of the late Tom Fleetwood, director of the Southern California Darts Association, who came up with the format in the late 1960s, ably abetted by his wife, Della.

Like the *News of the World,* the NAODT men's singles and doubles took the form of the best of three legs, but unlike the *News of the World,* the game was 301 and a double was required to both start and finish. Such a format leaves no margin for error. If a player does not hit that starting double very quickly, then the leg is pretty much lost. If a player reached the double before his opponent, he often had to hit the winning double within three darts or risk losing the leg. Such was the pressure of its short format. For every leg played, regardless of who won the previous leg, players always threw for the cork to decide who started first in the next leg. Concentration was vital in the NAODT, since one slip could consign a player to the spectators' seats for the remainder of the competition.

The Brits did not arrive to contest the NAODT until 1974 and were unpleasantly surprised to find the competition much stiffer than they had confidently predicted; they only claimed victory in the doubles competition. World Champion John Lowe described the NAODT as "the hardest and most difficult one to win"—more difficult than the *News of the World* title.

At the start of the twenty-first century, the format of the NAODT was changed to the best of three games of 501 and this initially proved unpopular with the players. However, today the NAODT has been reestablished as one of the most important tournaments on the world darting calendar.

WINMAU World Masters

The WINMAU World Masters is the longest continually running "world" title.

In 1974, the British record company Phonogram sponsored the first two World Masters. (The WINMAU Dartboard Company took over the sponsorship in 1976.) The World Masters was known for having no seeded players and forcing all competitors to fight it out through tough preliminary rounds. However, in 2007, the organizers changed the rules and allowed the eight top-ranked men's players to qualify automatically for places in the last sixteen. (Somewhat peculiarly, this change did not apply to the Women's World Masters.)

The migration of top players to the PDC to play in that organization's tournaments (the World Masters is run under the auspices of the BDO) has raised questions about the validity of the World Masters as an indicator of world-class darts. However, the recent Masters competitions have seen no reduction in the quality of the play or the averages scored, the statistics comparing well with those attained in PDC competitions.

Lakeside (formerly the Embassy) World Professional Darts Championship

When sixteen British and international darts players were invited by the BDO to attend the inaugural Embassy World Professional Darts Championship in 1978, no one could have predicted that the competition would grow stronger and still be contested more than thirty years later.

In 1985, this jewel in the crown of the BDO was held for the first time at the Lakeside Country Club, Frimley Green, Surrey, England, where it is still hotly contested today. In 2004, the Lakeside Country Club became the title sponsor of this prestigious event. It has become every serious darts player's dream to step up onto the stage at Lakeside (which is known within the darting fraternity as the "Home of Darts") and play in a World Professional Darts Championship final.

PDC World Darts Championship

This organization and this championship, with its razzmatazz and cacophony of sound, dragged the sport of darts (whether we liked it or not) kicking and screaming into the twenty-first century.

When the sixteen "rebel" darts players broke away from the BDO after the 1993 Embassy World Professional Darts Championship, their allegiance thereafter would be to the World Darts Council (WDC), later to be known as the Professional Darts Corporation (PDC). Skeptics said that an "alternative" world championship would never take place. The skeptics were proved wrong when, in January 1994, twenty-four top players from around the world lined up at the Circus Tavern, Purfleet, Essex, England, to contest the inaugural Skol World Championship with every player targeting the £16,000 ($24,512) first prize. The winner of the first WDC World Championship was England's Dennis Priestley, who beat fellow Englishman Phil Taylor 6–1. Unfazed by Priestley's win, Taylor then took personal control of this new world championship and won it thirteen times between 1995 and 2010.

Broadcast on satellite TV, the finals were the first to introduce what the press described as "thrill-a-minute darting action amid colorful and noisy American-style glittering presentations." In terms of presentation, the WDC competition was everything the traditional BDO event was not or, perhaps more accurately, did not want to be. Scantily clad young women leading the "gladiators" out into the darts arena to the sound of loud, thumping music and the roar of the crowd was something that even the hardiest darts follower had not experienced before. A new era of darts had arrived.

LEGENDS OF THE GAME

RAYMOND VAN BARNEVELD (THE NETHERLANDS)

Born in Den Haag (The Hague) in the Netherlands in 1967, this former postal worker became a national hero when he won the Embassy World Professional Darts Championship in 1998 and then returned the following year to retain his title. He later added the 2003 and 2005 world titles and has become one of the most famous Dutch sports personalities of all time.

For many years, Barneveld and Phil Taylor, because of their allegiance to different darts organizations (Barneveld the BDO and Taylor the PDC), rarely played one another, and fans pressed hard for them to meet in competition to decide which of the two world champions was the *real* world champion. They met in a head-to-head, timed competition in 1999 that Taylor won twenty-one legs to ten, but this didn't prove much. It was not until Barneveld joined the PDC in February 2006 that he showed the darts world that he was capable of taking on Taylor. Barneveld rewarded his followers in 2007 when he won the Ladbrokes.com World Darts Championship, bringing to an end the long reign of "The Power."

Supported by hordes of fans known collectively as the "Orange Army," Barneveld (nicknamed both "Barney" and "The Man") has won numerous titles in his glittering and highly successful darts career, a career that continues unabated.

Web site (in Dutch): www.raymondvanbarneveld.nl

ERIC BRISTOW (ENGLAND)

Eric Bristow is by far the most recognizable face in darts, even though he has not won a major tournament for over a decade. Born in Stoke Newington, London, in 1957, Bristow was, as they say, in the right place at the right time. Bristow's rise to the top of the darts world was meteoric.

Love him or loathe him, the "Crafty Cockney," like Muhammad Ali in boxing, spoke loud and proud, and when he said he was going to achieve something he almost always succeeded. Overflowing with self-confidence, Bristow swept most, if not all, before him in the 1970s, 1980s, and early 1990s, winning the Embassy World Professional Darts Championship on five occasions (1980, 1981, 1984, 1985, and 1986). He was also the losing finalist in 1983 (losing to the 100–1 qualifier, England's Keith Deller), 1987, 1989, 1990 (where he lost to his protégé Phil Taylor), and 1991. Among his many hundreds of other tournament wins were five WINMAU World Masters titles in 1977, 1979, 1981, 1983, and 1984.

In the late 1980s, Bristow suddenly began to suffer from the darts player's nightmare ailment, "dartitis"—an affliction that manifests itself in the player being unable to let go of his dart.

For other players, the attack of "dartitis" might have spelled the end, but not for Bristow. Although he never really returned to top form, he stayed in the public eye through exhibitions and as a darts pundit for satellite TV. In 1989, Bristow's accomplishments in darts were recognized by the queen by the award of an MBE (Member of the Order of the British Empire), the only darts player to have his service to darts recognized in that way.

A prime mover, with fifteen other professional darts players, in the shift away from the BDO in the early 1990s to the-then World Darts Council (later the Professional Darts Corporation), Bristow remains much loved by the majority of darts fans, despite his decision to no longer compete in top tournaments.

Still a larger-than-life personality, the "Crafty Cockney" continues to take on all comers on the exhibition circuit. His contribution to the sport of darts is inestimable. It is unlikely that the game would be where it is today if Bristow had taken up bowling instead.

Web site: www.legendsofdarts.com

STACY BROMBERG (UNITED STATES)

Stacy has been the number one United States player sixteen out of the last eighteen years and has won the NAODT six consecutive times, from 1995 to 2000.

Probably the most successful women's United States darts player ever, in 2008 Stacy (born in Los Angeles in 1956) was ranked number one in the American Darts Organization (ADO) ranking points tables for the thirteenth consecutive year—and her sixteenth in total. In 2007, Stacy was also ranked number one in the American Darts Association (ADA) rankings and was the number one "Woman in the World" for the National Darts Association (NDA), the association governing electronic/soft-tip darts in the United States.

Now a Las Vegas resident, Stacy is still very much involved with the sport of darts, but is also recognized for her fundraising efforts for Make-A-Wish Foundation of Southern Nevada through her Darts Scores for Charity Foundation. It is for this reason that Stacy has earned the nick-name "The Wish Granter."

Web site: www.stacy.homestead.com

TONY DAVID (AUSTRALIA)

In 2002, Tony David became the first Australian to win the Embassy World Professional Darts Championship, but his success will be remembered for more than that.

David, known as the "Deadly Boomerang," was born in Townsville, Queensland, in 1967 and he first played darts in 1993. In 1997, he won the Queensland Singles and he went on to win many Australian championships.

But it is for his 2002 world championship win that David is best known. As a 50–1 outsider to win the 2002 Embassy, David swept all before him. However, as newspapers at the time reported, David had overcome more than his opponents to become world champion.

It was revealed that since birth David had suffered with arthritic hemophilia, a condition that meant that, among other things, he could not straighten his throwing arm and everyday bumps would cause large bruises. Such strength in the face of adversity made him a favorite with the Lakeside crowd.

Tony David is a prime example of beating the odds and living the dream that lesser folks would have deemed impossible.

Anastasia Dobromyslova (Russia)

Although born in Russia, Anastasia Dobromyslova, at the time of this writing, lives and plays her darts in Wales.

Born in 1984, Dobromyslova, who played her first darts at the age of eleven and has been the Russian women's darts champions six times, won the WINMAU World Girls' Masters in 2001 and signaled the darts world that she had world champion potential.

In 2006, Dobromyslova was the first Russian darts player to compete on the Lakeside World Championship stage. Her appearance at Lakeside was preceded by her winning the Scottish Open and the British Open Women's Singles and Pairs titles. In October 2006, Dobromyslova was a quarterfinalist in the WINMAU Women's World Masters.

In January 2008, Dobromyslova reached the final of the Lakeside Women's World Professional Darts Championship and convincingly beat the seven-time world champion, Trina Gulliver, two sets to one, to lift the women's world crown. Shortly afterwards, Dobromyslova joined the Professional Darts Corporation and was, therefore, unable to defend her world title in 2009.

Maureen Flowers (England)

Maureen Flowers was one of the most influential women darts players of the late 1970s and 1980s.

Born in 1946, Flowers had one of her first darting successes in 1975 when she was runner-up in the National Darts Association Women's Individual competition, winner of the Women's Pairs (with Yvonne Allen), and reached the last eight of the Mixed Pairs (with Harry Carhart).

Frequently throwing three-dart averages that were equal to the men, Flowers won hundreds of major titles, including four consecutive Denmark Opens (1980–1983), four consecutive Swedish Opens (1978–1981), the Finland Open twice (1985 and 1987), the British Open in 1982, and the North American Open Darts Tournament in 1977 and 1979. Flowers also captained her country's team on a number of occasions.

Although Flowers once told reporters that she started playing darts "as a joke," she became the face of women's international darts for more than a decade and did much to raise the profile of women's darts.

Bobby George (England)

England's Bobby George, born in 1945, is considered to be one of the most colorful, popular, and successful darts player in the history of the sport. He will frequently enter the stage—carrying a gold candelabra and wearing gold rings and other jewelry that catch the stage lights—to the sound of Queen's "We Are the Champions" and the cheers of hordes of loyal fans, cracking jokes as he goes.

Nearly thirty years old when he first took up the sport, George discovered that he had a natural talent for darts and in 1976 won the first singles event he entered. In 1977, he reached the quarterfinals of the prestigious WINMAU World Masters and in 1978 won his first major title, the North American Open Darts Tournament. He followed that success with victory in the *News of the World* Individual Darts Championship in 1979, a title he again claimed in the 1985–1986 season.

An Embassy World Professional Darts Championship finalist in 1980 against the eventual champion, Eric Bristow, and a quarterfinalist and a semifinalist in the following two Embassies, George firmly established himself as the people's champion. At the end of the 1980s, George, a natural entertainer, turned his main focus away from major tournaments and concentrated more on the lucrative exhibition circuit.

In 1994, despite sustaining a serious back injury in an earlier round, George reached the finals of the Embassy World Championship, but was beaten by Canadian John Part. Since then George has continued to play mainly exhibition darts, but has extended his portfolio by becoming a TV darts pundit for the BBC.

Web site: www.bobbygeorge.com

Trina Gulliver (England)

In January 2007, at the Lakeside Country Club, Trina "Golden Girl" Gulliver became women's world champion for the seventh consecutive year.

Born in 1969 in Warwickshire, Gulliver was encouraged to play darts from a very early age and was selected to play for her county a few months before her eighteenth birthday. After one season on the Warwickshire Ladies' "B" team, Gulliver was promoted to the "A" team and has stayed there ever since.

Gulliver fought hard to secure sponsorship to enable her to fulfill her dream of becoming a full-time darts professional and, in a sport that remains today very pub-oriented and male-centric, Gulliver succeeded against incredible odds.

In the late 1990s, Gulliver and other top women darts players pressed for their own world championship. This finally came to fruition with the introduction of the Embassy Women's World Darts Championship in 2001, a title Gulliver won in the inaugural year and retained for six subsequent years, losing for the first time in 2008 to Anastasia Dobromyslova. Gulliver reached the world final again in 2009, but was beaten by the Netherland's Francis Hoenselaar. However, in 2010, Gulliver regained her world title (her eighth) by beating Wales' Rhian Edwards two sets to 0.

Gulliver has won every major title in the sport of darts. Her record of seven successive wins in the Women's World Championship is unlikely to be equaled.

Web site: www.trinagulliver.net

DETA HEDMAN (ENGLAND)

Born in Jamaica in 1959 but now living in England, Deta Hedman was one of the world's best female darts players of the late 1980s and 1990s, and she has reemerged in the new millennium.

Winner of the Swiss Open four times (1989, 1991, 1992, and 1996), the Sweden Open four times (1990, 1991, 1992, and 1995), the Finland Open four times (1989, 1991, 1992, and 1996), and numerous other national and international titles, Hedman became WINMAU World Master in 1994. She also represented her country on multiple occasions in international competitions.

However, by 1997, Hedman, apparently disillusioned by the poor financial rewards and continual backbiting in women's darts, announced her retirement from the sport. After a decade as the top female darter, during which she had mentored other up-and-coming players, including Trina Gulliver, Hedman sought a life away from the darts circuit.

Hedman reappeared in 2002 on the PDC circuit. She found immediate success in Nevada in July 2002 when she won the first Las Vegas Desert Classic Women's Singles title. In 2009, Hedman returned to the BDO circuit with some measure of success, including qualifying for the Women's World Championship at Lakeside in 2010 (in which she reached the semi-finals) at the age of 50.

FRANCIS HOENSELAAR (THE NETHERLANDS)

Born in Rotterdam in 1965, Francis Hoenselaar took up the sport of darts when she was only seventeen. In 1988, she moved to Spain and quit the sport, only taking it up again when she returned home in 1990. She soon became the number one women's darts player in Holland. In 1991, Hoenselaar reached the semifinals of the WINMAU Women's World Masters, but lost to Sandy Reitan of the United States.

From that moment on, Hoenselaar was determined to win the Masters title, an ambition she realized in 1999 when she beat England's Trina Gulliver three games to one. During the final, both Hoenselaar and Gulliver averaged over thirty-one points per dart, an average higher than that scored in the men's final.

In the years that followed, there have been many more "clashes of the titans"—Hoenselaar versus Gulliver. Hoenselaar (known popularly as the "Dutch Crown") claimed the Masters again in 2006 and 2008. With hundreds of major titles under her belt, Hoenselaar finally reached her main goal in 2009: She defeated Gulliver for the Lakeside Women's World Championship title.

Web site (in Dutch): www.franciscahoenselaar.nl

JOHNNY KUCZYNSKI (UNITED STATES)

Born in 1973 in Pennsylvania, Johnny Kuczynski has, over the last few years, established himself as a top American and international darter, in both the soft-tip and steel-tip competitions.

"Johnny K" made his debut in the PDC World Championship in 2005 and made it through to the last sixteen, where England's Gary Welding defeated him. In the 2006 World Series of Darts, where thirty-two top PDC players took on the cream of U.S. steel-tip darters, Kuczynski was the only American darter to make it through to the second round with a sensational win over the-then twice world champion, Canada's John Part.

In September of 2006 Kuczynski made it to the last sixteen of the UK Open Welsh Regional Final (steel-tip) and then in 2007 became the Bullshooter Pro Singles (soft-tip) champion. That same year, with darts partner, Raymond van Barneveld, he won the World Darts Challenge. It was a memorable 14–11 win against countryman Ray Carver and his partner, the then thirteen-time world champion, Phil "The Power" Taylor.

Web site: www.johnnykdarts.com

JOHN LOWE (ENGLAND)

Born in 1945 in New Tupton, Derbyshire, England, and originally a carpenter by trade, John Lowe took up darts by accident in a local pub, when he was asked to step in for a player who had to answer an urgent call of nature. Lowe took the darts, won the match, and never looked back. He was twenty-one at the time.

Known as "Old Stoneface" because of his expressionless face when throwing his darts, Lowe has been one of the most consistent players of all time and has shared his experiences and his knowledge by writing five books since 1980. His autobiography, titled *Old Stoneface*, was published in 2005.

Lowe has won the Embassy World Darts Championship on three occasions (1979, 1987, and 1993). He is the only darts player to have won the world title in three different decades and the only player to have played in every world championship from 1978 to 2004. However, Lowe is probably best known as the first darts player to hit a televised nine-dart 501. (See "Darting Nirvana" on page 38.)

Although no longer chasing titles, Lowe still plays exhibition matches and tours with other legends of the game, including five-time World Champion Eric Bristow. A winner of over a thousand titles in his career, Lowe can legitimately lay claim to being one of the greatest darts players ever.

Web site: www.legendsofdarts.com

John Part (Canada)

John Part, born in Ontario in 1966, first played darts in 1987 when someone bought him a dartboard for Christmas.

Seven years later, while still a relative unknown in international darts, Part coolly and calmly beat the local hero, England's Bobby George, 6–0 to be crowned the 1994 Embassy World Darts champion. It was the first time the world title had gone to a player outside the UK. When he won the PDC World Championship title in 2001 in a close-fought 7–6 contest against Phil Taylor, Part became one of only a handful of players who have won the world championship under both the BDO and the PDC. In 2008, he secured his third world title at the Ladbroke.com World Darts Championship held in London.

Nicknamed "Darth Maple," Part is arguably the best darts player Canada has ever produced. He has shared his vast knowledge of the sport as a TV commentator and through a quality how-to series on his Web site.

Web site: www.partsdarts.com

Leighton Rees (Wales)

Born in Wales in 1940, Leighton Rees was a natural darts player and became one of the most respected professionals ever.

Rees was persuaded to go professional in 1976 and international success came the following year when he led the Welsh national team to victory in the first WDF World Cup, a tournament in which he also won the individual title.

On February 10, 1978, at the Heart of the Midlands nightclub, in Nottingham, England. Rees won the inaugural Embassy World Professional Darts Championship to become darts' first world champion. He defeated England's John Lowe in the final and collected the winner's check for £3,000 ($4,881).

Although becoming world champion was the pinnacle of his career, Rees continued to be a leading contender in all the major darts competitions he entered. His gentle manner and warm personality made him a great ambassador for darts the world over.

Despite failing health in the 1990s, he remained a popular character on the exhibition circuit. Adored by fellow professionals and fans alike, Rees, known as the "Gentleman of Darts," eventually succumbed to a long-term heart condition in June 2003.

PHIL TAYLOR (ENGLAND)

Born in 1960 in Tunstall, Stoke-on-Trent, into a world of poverty and hardship, Phil Taylor was destined to become, as the darts commentator and pundit Sid Waddell has said, "the greatest darts player ever to draw breath."

In the late 1980s, Taylor was spotted playing darts by five-time World Champion Eric Bristow. Bristow recognized great potential and became Taylor's mentor and sponsor. Taylor's professional career was kicked off in 1988 when, unranked, he beat the then-current World Champion Bob Anderson 5–1 in the Canadian Open and won $5,000. In 1990, Taylor entered fifty darts competitions and won forty-eight of them. One of these forty-eight tournaments was the 1990 Embassy World Professional Darts Championship, where Taylor met his mentor, Eric Bristow, in the final and beat him 6–1.

Initially known as the "Crafty Potter"—a nod of recognition to Bristow's "Crafty Cockney"—Taylor soon changed his nickname to "The Power." Taylor powered his way to fifteen world titles (up to 2010) and numerous other major tournament wins, including the *News of the World* Individual Darts Championship in 1997. In 2002, at the Stan James World Matchplay in Blackpool, England, he shot the first "live" (on satellite TV) televised nine-dart 501 and picked up £100,000 ($162,700).

With three-dart averages in excess of 100 (and often exceeding 110), Taylor was essentially invincible for nearly two decades, but in recent years he has been less successful (by his own very high personal standards). With more money in the sport and more young players coming up, Taylor's domination of the game was bound to be threatened. Some fans saw a few defeats as the end of "The Power." Taylor—described by *The Sun* newspaper as "Britain's greatest living sportsman"—did not see it that way. He regained his form, reclaimed the world title in 2009 and 2010, and is dominating the circuit once again.

Web site: www.philthepower.com

JAMES WADE (ENGLAND)

Of all the rising stars in professional darts, England's James Wade, a left-hander, is currently one of the sport's most outstanding prospects.

Born in 1983 in Aldershot, Hampshire, Wade learned to play darts with his father and grandfather at the age of fourteen.

In 2002, Wade won his first major title, the Swiss Open, and at the age of only twenty he was selected to play for his country. Continued success throughout 2003 and 2004 convinced Wade that he should join the professional ranks and he made the decision to join the PDC. In 2006, Wade hit an unprecedented three perfect nine-dart finishes in PDC-ranked events and rose to eleventh in the ranking table. In the summer of 2006, he reached the finals of the Stan James World Matchplay at Blackpool, but lost to Phil Taylor. Many darts pundits were sure that Wade was a great hope for the future of darts, provided he could stay focused. They were proved right as he returned to Blackpool in 2007 and won the World Matchplay.

With an ever-growing list of successes, Wade could be the brightest star of darts' next generation.

Web site: www.jameswade.co.uk

JOCKY WILSON (SCOTLAND)

One of the real characters of the darts world during the heady days of the mid-1970s to late-1980s, John Thomas ("Jocky") Wilson (born in 1950) first showed evidence of his darting skills when, in 1975 in his native Scotland, he won the Dryborough Doubles and the Fife Super League Singles. In 1978, he reached the finals of the first Europe Cup, yet he was uncertain whether or not he had any future in darts and, at that time, often thought about giving up darts altogether.

The good news for the sport was that he did not give up—not at that time anyway. He won the Embassy World Championship in 1982 and became the first Scottish world darts champion. Wilson flicked his darts rather than threw them. The whole action looked uncomfortable and unwieldy, yet was extremely successful, as was shown when he took his second Embassy World Championship title in 1989. However, fame and illness eventually took its toll; by 1996, Wilson, always a colorful and unpredictable character, had withdrawn from the sport completely.

Despite various attempts since then to persuade him to return to the oche, Wilson has refused and remains more or less a recluse in his home in Kirkcaldy, Scotland. Even though he has not thrown a dart in a major tournament for over a decade, Wilson remains one of the best-remembered stars of the Golden Age of darts.

In 2009, the Professional Darts Corporation announced that a new tournament was to be introduced named in honor of this great Scottish darts player. Named "The Jocky Wilson Cup," this is an England versus Scotland match where two nominated players from each country play both singles and doubles matches in a similar format to Davis Cup tennis.

In terms of equipment, there is, of course, much more to darts than just a set of three darts and a dartboard.

This chapter looks briefly at equipment that will help darts players improve their game. Therefore, darts mugs, plates, badges, watches, clocks, card games, beanie hats, T-shirts, "Darts players do it three in a bed" bumper stickers, witty darts underwear, and the like will only receive mention in this paragraph. Such items are "for amusement only."

None of the accessories mentioned in this chapter will help at all if you choose to ignore the "How to Play" and related chapters in this book. Purchasing these items will *not* make you into a great player. Still, these items may *assist* in the process. Here, then, are some of the most important items for both the casual and the serious darter.

FLIGHTS

Dart flights have come a long way since the paper and turkey feather flights of the first half of the twentieth century. Nowadays, few paper or feather flights are seen on the oche, since 99.9 percent of darters use "plastic" flights made from polypropylene. Figure 17 shows some of the most common flight shapes. The most popular, not surprisingly, is known as the "standard" flight and is similar to the shape that was more or less standard for paper flights in the 1940s and '50s.

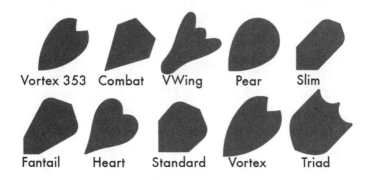

Vortex 353 Combat VWing Pear Slim

Fantail Heart Standard Vortex Triad

Figure 17

Flights come in an endless variety: There are plain flights and dimpled flights, flights with holograms, rude flights, pretty flights, flights advertising your favorite alcoholic beverage, and so on. You can even have your own personalized flights made for a few dollars. Most of the top darts equipment manufacturers produce a pack that contains various types of flights for darters to experiment with. While these do not cover the full range of available flights, they do offer a chance to see if a particular kind of flight improves your game.

Once you have found a flight shape that works well for you, stick with it.

One other flight-related accessory available is the "flight protector" or "flight saver." These are small metal or plastic caps that fit snugly over the exposed end of each dart flight and prevent damage from following darts. In this way, they prolong the life of each flight. However useful these items may be, they do not protect the flights from bad handling by the player.

SHAFTS

The earliest wooden darts ("French darts") were one piece, so there was no separate shaft. With the advent of brass-barreled darts came the cane shaft and later plastic and metal shafts. Today, shafts (also called "stems") are mainly made from plastic, ultrastrong nylon, aluminum, or titanium.

Again, as with dart flights, the range of shafts is extensive. Shafts are available in various lengths, colors, and designs. Some have rotating aluminum tops (to reduce flight deflection of an incoming dart), while others are described as "flexible," meaning the plastic or nylon material is soft and bends with the impact of a following dart.

To give you a range of options, manufacturers include in their packs various shafts and flights. These are designed to help you refine your throw and improve your overall game by allowing you to experiment with different combinations of shaft and flight.

Dart retailers sell small rings that fit between the barrel and the shaft and lock the shaft in place. No matter how effective this shaft lock might be, check the tightness of the shafts before throwing your darts.

NONSLIP FINGER WAX

In the old days, when a darts player's hands became sweaty, the solution was to rub chalk on the dart barrels or the player's hands (or both). But that led to another problem: chalk residue on the face of the dartboard. So a solution had to be found and that was "finger wax," nonslip wax that gives a better grip, yet leaves no visible residue on either the dart or the dartboard.

CHECK-OUT TABLES

Also known as a list of outshots—an example can be seen in Appendix B—check-out tables are generally far too big for a player to copy and take along to a darts match. The secret, of course, is to *learn* all the outshots. Until that happens, all major darts suppliers produce pocket-size check-out tables that feature the standard ways to finish a game in two or three darts. The chart in Appendix B can also be downloaded free-of-charge from my Web site www.patrickchaplin.com.

If you're in any doubt, carry a copy with you and refer to it before and during the game, as necessary—and do not be embarrassed if you do because it is all part of the learning process. You will soon be leaving it at home.

DARTS SCORERS

Darts was originally scored on a cribbage board, but as soon as it became more popular, the blackboard and chalk were introduced and later the pen and dry-erase whiteboard.

Electronic scorers allow you to set the score to, say, 501, for both players or teams. Then each individual score is punched into the keyboard, another button is pressed, and the sum is instantly deducted from the current total. This is all the basic electronic scorer does, but the more sophisticated versions include the capability of recovering all previous scores and producing three-dart averages.

With soft-tip darts, these features, and so many more, are built into the machines. A "chalker" (the person recording scores by chalk in the traditional game) is redundant, and there is no need to punch in scores. Some electronic darts machines can be linked to a national database, so that at the end of an evening of league competition every player and every team can find out their average and their team position in the league before they go home.

In many major steel-tip tournaments, you will still see a "caller" (or referee who calls out each individual score) and "markers" (one for each of the two competing players), though there are electronic displays for those in the audience. However, there are a few signs that the callers and markers are gradually being replaced by computer technology.

DARTS WALLET AND CASES

Almost all quality sets of modern darts come complete with a leather, leatherette, or tough plastic wallet or case in which to keep your arrows safe. With most darts breaking down into three handy pieces (point and barrel, shaft, and flight), they fit neatly into a wallet or case, which fits equally neatly into a player's pocket or handbag.

Always keep your darts wallet with you, secure in your pocket while playing or resting. For some players, losing their personal darts loses them the match.

DARTS: ADDING WEIGHT

One of the more unusual darts items produced in recent years is called, in at least one darts catalogue, "addagram." These small, one-gram brass weights simply screw into the barrel of a dart and thus add weight.

This may be useful if a player wishes to experiment with a heavier dart, but cannot afford to buy another set. In fact, more than one of these small brass pieces can be added, but the problem is that they also add *length* to the dart. Players should make allowances for that added length when they throw.

EARPLUGS

No, this is not a joke.

One of the noticeable differences between the behavior of darts fans at tournaments twenty years ago and today is that the crowds have become much noisier. Modern crowds have little or no respect for the players on the oche and talk, laugh, cheer, and heckle all the time—even when the players are throwing their darts.

Crowds in excess of two thousand are becoming commonplace at darts tournaments in the UK, and at times the cacophony of sound can become unbearable for the players. World Champion Raymond van Barneveld has resorted to plugs on occasion. If you become a serious tournament player and the noise gets to you, you may want to consider plugging things up.

PERSONALIZED MERCHANDISE

Personalized flights and shafts can be inexpensive and may provide a morale boost (or at least a good laugh). Personalized darts tend to be more expensive than their mass-produced counterparts, but there are plenty of small companies that will make a set of darts to your specifications for around $60. Also, many companies produce customized dartboards both for corporate advertising and personal promotion. Check out the major manufacturers first or search the Internet.

The following selection of Web sites makes a great starting point:

United States

    Arachnid—www.bullshooter.com

    Bottelsen Darts—www.bottelsendarts.com

    Dart World—www.dartworld.com

    DMI Sports—www.dmisports.com

    Horizon Laser Darts—www.laserdarts.com

    Voks darts—www.voksdarts.com

United Kingdom

    Harrows Darts Technology—www.harrowsdarts.com

    Unicorn—www.unicorn-darts.com

    WINMAU Dartboard Company—www.winmau.com

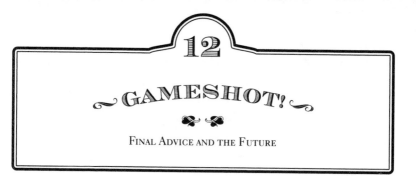

12

~ GAMESHOT! ~

FINAL ADVICE AND THE FUTURE

Using the information in this book, you will be able to reach the point of playing darts well. As I have stressed throughout, dedication, concentration, analysis of failures (and wins), and practice, practice, practice are clearly at the core of every successful player's game. If your game falters, realize that all darts players—both great and not-so-great—have off days, off weeks, off months, or even off years. But if you work at the game, no matter what your level, the rewards will come.

Take a lesson from multitime World Champion Phil "The Power" Taylor. In January 2007, Taylor lost his world title to Dutchman Raymond van Barneveld. It was one of the best darts matches ever seen. When he lost, many of his fans believed that this was the end of Taylor's reign as the world's best. He was later quoted as saying, "I know exactly what was wrong and I've not been dedicated . . . I wasn't concentrating . . . ." Phil picked himself up, refocused, practiced harder and longer, and started winning again—time after time.

Darts has come a long way from its origins in the spit-and-sawdust, noisy, male-dominated, smoke-filled, and beer-fumed English public bar of the nineteenth century. It is now played worldwide from the UK to the United States and Canada, from Iceland to Tonga, and from New Zealand to Switzerland. In fact, it is difficult to think of any country today where darts is not played in one form or another.

During the forthcoming decade, China, India, the Philippines, and Iran are all expected to affirm their status as hotbeds of darts. Some darts pundits anticipate that any of these four countries are capable of producing a world champion sooner rather than later. The world of darts is also continuing to keep a close eye on other countries, including the United States and Canada, which are consistently producing top darters to challenge the world's best. Across the board, standards of play and three-dart averages continue to improve, and more and more players are enjoying the sport of darts at all levels.

The bottom line for most darts players is enjoyment, and their enjoyment is enhanced by playing well. It is hoped that you have enjoyed this book and learned a lot more about what is arguably the most sociable and most popular sport in the world—at any level.

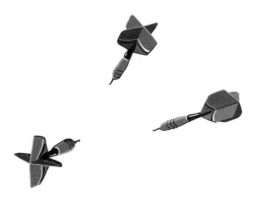

Appendix A

SINGLES, DOUBLES, AND TRIPLES COMBINATION CHART

Single	Double or two Singles	Single & Double or one Triple or three Singles	Two Doubles or Single & Triple or two Singles & Double	Single & two Doubles, or Triple & two Singles, or Triple & Double	Single, Double & Triple, or two Triples or three Doubles	Two Triples & Single or Triple & two Doubles	Two Triples & Double	Three Triples (Maximum)
1	2	3	4	5	6	7	8	9
2	4	6	8	10	12	14	16	18
3	6	9	12	15	18	21	24	27
4	8	12	16	20	24	28	32	36
5	10	15	20	25	30	35	40	45
6	12	18	24	30	36	42	48	54
7	14	21	28	35	42	49	56	63
8	16	24	32	40	48	56	64	72
9	18	27	36	45	54	63	72	81
10	20	30	40	50	60	70	80	90
11	22	33	44	55	66	77	88	99
12	24	36	48	60	72	84	96	108
13	26	39	52	65	78	91	104	117
14	28	42	56	70	84	98	112	126
15	30	45	60	75	90	105	120	135
16	32	48	64	80	96	112	128	144
17	34	51	68	85	102	119	136	153
18	36	54	72	90	108	126	144	162
19	38	57	76	95	114	133	152	171
20	40	60	80	100	120	140	160	180

Appendix B

OUTSHOT CHART

THREE DART FINISHES				THREE DART FINISHES				THREE DART FINISHES			
Score	1st Dart	2nd Dart	3rd Dart	Score	1st Dart	2nd Dart	3rd Dart	Score	1st Dart	2nd Dart	3rd Dart
170	T20	T20	Bull	149	T20	T19	D16	128	T18	T14	D16
169	---No outshot---			148	T20	T20	D12	127	T20	T17	D8
168	---No outshot---			147	T20	T17	D18	126	T19	T19	D6
167	T20	T19	Bull	146	T20	T18	D16	125	25	T20	D20
166	---No outshot---			145	T20	T15	D20	124	T20	T16	D8
165	---No outshot---			144	T20	T20	D12	123	T19	T16	D9
164	T20	T18	Bull	143	T20	T17	D16	122	T18	T20	D4
163	---No outshot---			142	T20	T14	D20	121	T17	T10	D20
162	---No outshot---			141	T20	T19	D12	120	T20	20	D20
161	T20	T17	Bull	140	T20	T16	D16	119	T19	T10	D16
160	T20	T20	D20	139	T19	T14	D20	118	T20	18	D20
159	---No outshot---			138	T20	T18	D12	117	T20	17	D20
158	T20	T20	D19	137	T19	T16	D16	116	T20	16	D20
157	T20	T19	D20	136	T20	T20	D8	115	T20	15	D20
156	T20	T20	D18	135	T20	T17	D12	114	T20	14	D20
155	T20	T19	D19	134	T20	T14	D16	113	T20	13	D20
154	T20	T18	D20	133	T20	T19	D8	112	T20	12	D20
153	T20	T19	D18	132	T20	T16	D12	111	T20	19	D16
152	T20	T20	D16	131	T20	T13	D16	110	T20	18	D16
151	T20	T17	D20	130	T20	20	Bull	109	T19	20	D16
150	T20	T18	D18	129	T19	T16	D12	108	T20	16	D16

OUTSHOT CHART

THREE DART FINISHES				TWO DART FINISHES			TWO DART FINISHES		
Score	1st Dart	2nd Dart	3rd Dart	Score	1st Dart	2nd Dart	Score	1st Dart	2nd Dart
107	T19	18	D16	100	T20	D20	79	T13	D20
106	T20	14	D16	98	T20	D19	78	T18	D12
105	T19	16	D16	97	T19	D20	77	T19	D10
104	T18	18	D16	96	T20	D18	76	T20	D8
103	T20	3	D20	95	T19	D19	75	T17	D12
102	T20	10	D16	94	T18	D20	74	T14	D16
101	T20	1	D20	93	T19	D18	73	T19	D8
99	T19	10	D16	92	T20	D16	72	T16	D12
				91	T17	D20	71	T13	D16
				90	T20	D15	70	T10	D20
				89	T19	D16	69	T15	D12
				88	T16	D20	68	T20	D4
				87	T17	D18	67	T17	D8
				86	T18	D16	66	T10	D18
				85	T15	D20	65	T19	D4
				84	T20	D12	64	T16	D8
				83	T17	D16	63	T13	D12
				82	T14	D20	62	T10	D16
				81	T19	D12	61	T15	D8
				80	T20	D10	60	20	D20

"501" game can be completed in 9 darts—180, 180, 141
For fun, try this combination: T20, T19, Bull (Three Times!) www.Darts501.com

APPENDIX C

DARTS GLOSSARY

Many of the words and phrases included in this glossary are used in this book. Others are a little less common, but will occasionally crop up during darts matches. Still others have been included because they are just plain *weird*. A few examples of the hundreds of colorful and quirky phrases derived from Cockney rhyming slang are also included, just in case you hear them when you're playing darts in a pub in the East End of London next time you take a trip "across the pond"!

In 1946 in his novel *Brensham Village,* English author John Moore described the language of darts as "its own esoteric terminology, some of which is common to the whole country and some of which is probably local. It is a language of association, with a bit of rhyming slang mixed up in it."

Fair enough, John. Game on!

against the darts A player is said to have won his game "against the darts" if his opponent threw first. If the player who throws first wins, then that game is said to have gone "with the darts."

arrows Slang term for darts, which makes a (tenuous) link between modern darts and archery.

bag o' nuts An English term for a score of 45. In early fairground darts stalls, the customer usually had to hit a score of "more than 45" to win a prize. For 45 and under, the customer received a consolation prize of a bag of nuts.

barrel The main body of the dart assembly, sometimes made of wood or brass, but nowadays mainly of tungsten, which is gripped by the player.

basement A general expression for the area at the bottom of a dartboard around the position of the double 3. The word is also used, occasionally, to actually mean double 3.

bed A section of a number.

bed and breakfast An English term for a score of 26. This is a common score, since the 1 and 5 sections are on either side of the 20. The expression is based on the price of staying in a bed-and-breakfast in Britain in the early twentieth century, when it cost two shillings and sixpence, thus "two and six."

beehives Cockney rhyming slang for "two fives" (double 5).

bogey number The numbers under 170 that cannot be finished in three darts: 169, 168, 166, 165, 163, 162, and 159. Also, the only number under 100 that cannot be finished in two darts: 99.

bounce-out The situation where a dart hits the wire spider or another dart and bounces off the dartboard.

brush A game in which a player finishes on a double before his opponent even gets a starting double. *Whitewash, skunked,* and *tin hat* are other terms for this embarrassing situation.

bull's-eye The center of the dartboard. It is divided into an outer ring, which is the "outer bull" or "single bull" worth 25 points. The inner ring is the "inner bull" or "double bull" worth 50 points. In the United States it's often called the "cork," and in England it may be called a "dosser," "pug," or "button."

bull-up Two players throw one dart each at the bull's-eye. The person whose dart is nearest to the center of the dartboard throws first in the game. Also called "shooting for cork" or "shooting for bull."

bust(ed) Scoring more points than you need to finish an "01" game. Your turn ends and you revert to the score you had at the beginning of the turn. However, *see* **no bust**.

caller An official at a darts tournament or league match who calls out the individual scores so that they can be recorded on the scoreboard by the "chalker." The caller is often also the referee and settles any disputes.

chalker The scorer in a game of steel-tip darts. Traditionally, this involved writing the scores in chalk on a blackboard, but the name has carried forward to other forms of manual recording, such as pen and whiteboard.

check out The player has completed the game and "checked out." For example, if a player has scored T20, T20, D10 to win the match, he has a "check out" of 140 points.

chucker A player who cannot throw properly and merely hurls his darts at the dartboard in the hope that they might score something.

clickety click A score of 66.

Come out! A cry heard when a player busts his score on his first or second dart, but carries on with his turn. Any additional darts thrown are seen to be extra practice.

cork The bull's-eye.

cover shot Your intended target (say triple 20) is obscured from all angles by your first or second dart, so the player goes for the next highest score attainable (triple 19).

dart(s) court A name for the overall area within which a game of darts is played.

dartitis "A state of nervousness which prevents a player from releasing a dart at the right moment when throwing" (Oxford English Dictionary).

diddle (or **middle for diddle**) Throwing one dart at the bull's-eye to see which player or team starts the game. *See* **bull-up.**

dirty darts A derogatory term used to describe tactics (such as excessive scoring in cricket) when the game is already well won. *See also* **point monger.**

double The outer ring of the dartboard. Shooting a dart into this ring scores double the value of the segment.

double bull The inner portion of the bull's-eye, also known as the "double cork" or "inner bull."

double in An "01" game in which the player must hit a double, any double, to begin scoring.

double out An "01" game in which the player must hit a double to reduce his score to exactly zero. Most "01" games require a double out.

double top Double 20. Also called "tops" or "top of the house."

double trouble Being unable to hit the necessary double, particularly the winning double.

eights A slang term in cricket for 18s.

exhibition A show featuring a top darts player (or players), which usually takes the form of the public taking on the player(s) in a single game of 501 or 701. This type of event is much more common and popular in the UK than in the United States.

fallout Scoring with a dart while aiming for another number (e.g., hitting a scorable 18 in cricket when shooting for a 20).

fat The largest part of a segment on a standard dartboard between the triple and the double. Players throwing for the "fat" part are usually assured a safe single.

feathers An English term for a score of 33. Apparently, it is derived from the Cockney expression "Firty-free fousand fevers on a frush's froat." Translation: "Thirty-three thousand feathers on a thrush's throat."

finishing double The double required to win the game or match.

fives A slang term in cricket for 15s.

flight The "feathers" that make a dart more stable and aerodynamic.

Game on! The usual announcement by the referee at the beginning of a game. It also serves as a request for silence.

gameshot The winning shot.

garden gates Cockney rhyming slang for either "two eights" (double 8) or a score of 88.

get the odd off The player has an odd number left and needs to make it even with his next dart in order to leave a finishing double.

good group (or **good grouping**) A compliment for a tight, accurate grouping of three darts.

hockey The original name of the throw line. Named after the "hockey line," which was a line used in pub games that existed before darts. Possibly derived from the old northern English word *hocken,* meaning "to spit." *See* **oche**.

house darts An unseemly and usually odd set of darts provided by a bar for those players who cannot be bothered to provide their own darts.

house rules In some places, particularly in the UK, darts continues to be played according to "house rules." The length of **oche** may be different, the **no bust** rule may apply, or every game might be **double in**. It is therefore advisable for any darts tourist to learn the house rules before playing against the locals.

inner bull *See* **bull's-eye**.

leg One game in a match or set. For example, a set may be the best of five legs, so the first player to win three legs (games) wins the set.

level pegging An English term for when the score is tied, after the "pegging" of a game of cribbage on a cribbage board.

loop The endorsed space of certain numbers on the metal ring of the dartboard (20, 18, 4, 6, 10, 19, 16, 8, 14, and 9). Used as a target in some unorthodox games.

madhouse Double 1 needed to win a game of "01." So called because the "madhouse" is a place most people do not want to be.

married man's side The left-hand side of the dartboard, where it is easier to hit a reasonable score without the risk of hitting small numbers, such as 1, 2, or 3. So named because the married man "always plays it safe."

maximum A score of 180, composed of three triple 20s. It is the highest score possible with three darts.

Mugs away! A traditional expression, meaning that the loser of the last game throws first in the next game.

nearest and farthest A method of determining teams when, say, four people are playing. All four throw one dart each at the bull's-eye and the player whose dart is nearest the bull pairs up with the player whose dart is farthest away.

nine-darter The perfect game of 501 completed in just nine darts. It doesn't get any better than this!

nines A slang term in cricket for 19s.

no bust Under some house rules, a player can score on the one or two darts that precede the dart that made him bust. (Under the normal **bust** rule, no darts for that turn would count.)

oche Another name for the throw line. Originally called **hockey**, the spelling was changed in the 1970s, probably to avoid confusion with the game of hockey. Pronounced "ockey"—like hockey without the "h."

off the island Any dart that has entirely missed the scoring area of the dartboard.

old hens Cockney rhyming slang for "two tens" (double 10).

outer bull *See* **bull's-eye**.

out (also **outshot**) Any number that can be scored in one, two, or three darts to complete a game.

perfect game A game that's won with the minimum number of darts: 501 in nine darts, 301 in six darts, cricket in eight darts.

pie (or **wedge**) The standard dartboard is divided into twenty segments, numbered 1 to 20. Any one of these segments can also be called a "pie" or a "wedge."

point monger In cricket, a "point monger" is a player who, even though he or she sees that the game is well won, insists on continuing to score excessively.

ranking event Any major darts event in which top finishers are awarded "ranking points."

red bit Although there are numerous "red bits" on the board, when a player says he is shooting for the "red bit," he invariably means the triple 20.

right there! An encouraging comment to a player who has just missed his intended target.

Robin Hood When a dart sticks into the shaft or flight of a dart already in the board.

round of nine A perfect round in any game (but especially cricket) where three triples are scored. For example, the perfect start of a cricket game would be triple 20, triple 19, triple 18: a round of nine.

Route 66 A score of 66. May also result in a brief rendition of this most famous of songs about the most famous of highways.

segment Any of the areas of the dartboard numbered 1 to 20 that score points.

set In a tournament, a player must achieve a given number of sets (composed of an agreed-upon number of **legs**) to win the match. Thus, in a match of the best of twenty-five sets, the first player to achieve thirteen sets is declared the winner.

sevens A slang term in cricket for 17s.

shaft The part of the dart that screws into the barrel of the dart and holds the flight in place. Also known as the "stem."

shanghai Hitting a single, double, and triple of the same number in one turn. In some games, this is an automatic win. Also the name of a game (see chapter 4).

shooter Term for a darts player, mostly used in the United States.

sixes A slang term in cricket for 16s.

spider The metal framework that separates each segment of the dartboard.

splash (or splashing) To throw two darts at a time, often with the opposite hand. Both darts must score in order for the throw to count. High and low splash scores are often used to determine partners before a game. In some games, a splash is used to determine the first score to beat.

split When a player leaves an odd number when going for a double. For example, if a player hits a single 5 when going for the double 5, he is said to have "five to split." That is, he must use another dart to create a double that can win the game.

split the 11 To throw a dart between the digits of the number 11 on the dartboard's number ring. May be used as a method to automatically win in some friendly games.

straight in An "01" game that doesn't require a player to hit a double to start scoring. This is more typical than games that are **double in**.

Sunset Strip A score of 77. For those old enough to remember the TV series *77 Sunset Strip,* starring Efrem Zimbalist Jr. and Edd "Kookie" Byrnes.

take chalks Score a game of darts with chalk on a blackboard in order to play the next game. (The winner stays on the oche until beaten.)

three in a bed Three darts in the same number. Often, more specifically, three darts in the same section of a number (i.e., three singles, doubles, or triples).

throw line The line behind which players must stand to throw their darts. Also known as the **oche** or **hockey**.

ton A score of 100. It possibly derives from early darters striking the bunghole of a beer barrel (known as a "tun") and scoring 100, the maximum score in archery. Scores over 100 are often referred to as "ton-x" as in "ton-forty" for 140 and "ton-eighty" for 180. A ton is usually written as a "T" on the scoreboard.

treble UK term for **triple**.

triple The inner ring of the dartboard, between the double ring and the outer bull's-eye. Scores three times the number.

trombones A score of 76. A nod to the song "76 Trombones" featured in the popular musical *The Music Man.*

turn A player's throw of three darts constitutes a turn. (A turn can be shorter than three darts if a player wins or busts on the first or second dart.)

two trees Cockney rhyming slang for "two threes" (double 3).

wedge *See* **pie**

Wet feet! An ancient cry in English pubs to indicate that the player has his feet over the throw line.

white horse Scoring three different triples in one turn in cricket. Some add the extra requirement that the triples must not have been previously registered in the game by you or your team.

wrong bed When a dart lands in an unintended segment.

X This is often used on a scoreboard to indicate that the player has double one left. The "X" is also used in games such as cricket to indicate two hits toward closing a number.

APPENDIX D

FURTHER READING AND OTHER RESOURCES

For those interested in learning more about the great sport of darts, this Appendix features an annotated list of recommended books and other resources.

Many of the publications mentioned are long out of print but, thanks to the Internet, most can be found via Web sites such as www.abebooks.com. The only Web site currently specializing in secondhand darts books is my own: www.patrickchaplin.com.

DARTS HISTORY

Brown, Derek. *The Guinness Book of Darts*. Enfield: Guinness Superlatives Ltd., 1982. This book is still one of the best introductions to the modern game.

Chaplin, Patrick. *Darts in England 1900–1939: A Social History*. Manchester: Manchester University Press, 2009. This is the first comprehensive social history of darts in England and is essential reading for scholars wishing to further research the sport.

Croft-Cooke, Rupert. *Darts*. London: Geoffrey Bles, 1936. The first book entirely devoted to darts, this is an interesting sketch of darts in England during the "boom" of the late 1930s.

McClintock, Jack. *The Book of Darts*. New York: Random House, 1977. Both a history book and a how-to book, this remains one of the best darts books to come out of the United States.

Peek, Dan William. *To the Point: The Story of Darts in America*. Rocheport, MO: Pebble Publishing Inc., 2001. Using some extraordinary sources, Peek recounts the history of the sport in the United States. An excellent foundation for further research into U.S. darts history.

Waddell, Sid. *Bellies and Bullseyes: The Outrageous True Story of Darts*. London: Ebury Press, 2007. Waddell has been involved with televised darts from the early 1970s. This book offers his personal insights into darts both on and off TV over more than three decades.

DARTS BIOGRAPHIES AND AUTOBIOGRAPHIES

Brown, Derek. *The Crafty Cockney: The Official Biography of Eric Bristow.* London: Queen Anne Press, 1985. A biography of five-time World Champion Eric Bristow, one of the best-known faces in darts. This book was published after the third of his five Embassy world title wins. Bristow has since published his autobiography, titled *The Crafty Cockney* (London: Century, 2008), which completes his story.

Gulliver, Trina (with Patrick Chaplin). *Golden Girl: The Autobiography of the Greatest Ever Ladies' Darts Player.* London: John Blake, 2008. The author is a seven-time Lakeside Women's World Professional Darts Champion (2001–2007). The first autobiography written by a female darts player, this book illustrates just how difficult it is for women to succeed in darts at the highest level.

Lowe, John (with Patrick Chaplin). *Old Stoneface: The Autobiography of Britain's Greatest Darts Player.* London: John Blake, 2005. Revised and expanded paperback edition (London: John Blake, 2009). After more than thirty years as a professional darts player, Lowe reveals the trials and tribulations of a life "in darts."

Taylor, Phil (with Sid Waddell). *The Power: My Autobiography.* London: CollinsWillow, 2003. Revised and updated paperback edition (London: CollinsWillow, 2004). Taylor is considered the greatest darts player of all time.

DARTS LEAGUES

There are no darts books published to date that include advice about setting up a darts league. An Internet search should yield enough information, and a great place to start is the Crow's Darts Web site (www.crowsdarts.com).

DARTS INSTRUCTION AND ETIQUETTE

Brackin, Ivan and William Fitzgerald. *All About Darts: America's Most Complete and Up-to-Date Book on the Game of Darts.* Chicago: Contemporary Books, 1986. Published over twenty years ago, this book remains a great introduction to the game.

Carey, Chris. *The American Darts Organization Book of Darts,* rev. ed. New York: Lyons Press, 2005. Carey's work features equipment, techniques, and games, together with tips from American pros Stacy Bromberg and Steve Brown. An indispensable book—essential reading.

Everson, Capt. Fred. *A Bar Player's Guide to Winning Darts.* Victoria, British Columbia: Trafford, 2002. Though written in an extremely casual manner, this book manages to get all the important points across.

Goodwin, E. Irene. *Ways to Go—'01 Outs.* Self-published, 2003. A handy, pocket-sized, plastic-coated outshot chart.

Holmes, Fred H. *Darts American Style.* Dallas: Lone Star, 1989. Holmes examines the American approach to darts and includes references to the distinct "American board," which differs from the standard board.

Lowe, John. *The Art of Darts.* London: Hodder and Stoughton, 2009. The three-time World Professional Darts champion presents a master class for darts players, plus a bonus master class on how to become a professional player.

Mahoney, John. *Good Darts.* Fort Collins: Black Swan, 1991. An excellent tutorial book with all sorts of alternative games.

McLeod, Robert and Jay D. Cohen. *Darts Unlimited.* New York: Grosset and Dunlap, 1977. A great introductory book for all players about all aspects of the game.

Orav, Mike. *Become Your Darts: An Enlightening Guide to Better Darting.* Self-published, 1988. The reader is led through all the fundamentals of the sport via Orav's snappy, witty, and direct text and the excellent illustrations by Jay Zimmerman.

Prokop, Dave, ed. *The Dart Book.* Mountain View, California: World Publications, 1978. This fine introductory book includes articles by a number of well-known U.S. darters and organizers.

Silberzahn, George. *Darts Beginning to End.* Self-published, 2009. Silberzahn has written extensively on darts for a number of years. This book reflects his vast experience and includes a series of short biographies on male and female U.S. darts players.

HUMOR AND REPORTAGE

Brandreth, Gyles. *The Little Red Darts Book.* London: The Bodley Head, 1978. This is a clever collection of observations on darts traditions, players, and variations of the game, all illustrated by English cartoonist Larry (real name Terence Parkes).

Brockwell, Norma. *101 Excuses for Bad Darts,* 3rd ed. Self-published, 2005. Originally published in Australia in 1983, this book of darts cartoons has withstood the test of time.

D'Egville, Alan and Geoffrey. *Darts with the Lid Off.* London: Cassell, 1938. The first humorous book on darts. It was created to raise funds for British voluntary hospitals.

George, Bobby. *Scoring for Show: Doubles for Dough—Bobby's Darts Lingo.* Studley: Know the Score Books, 2010. A humorous approach to the unique language of darts by one of Britain's most popular professional darts players.

Seigel, Paul. *It's a Funny Game, Darts. Life. The Best of Dartoid's World.* Columbia MO: Totem Pointe, 2005. A famous—some might say "infamous"—darts fanatic and syndicated darts journalist, Paul Seigel (aka "Dartoid") travels around the globe in search of the sport. This book is a compilation of some of his best columns.

SOFT-TIP DARTS

Bucci, Timothy R. *A Quiver of Three: Soft-Tip Darts for the New Player.* Bloomington, Indiana: AuthorHouse, 2005. This is an excellent soft-tip manual for both new and experienced players.

Holmes, Fred H. *Electronic (Soft-Tip) Darts: The American Revolution.* Dallas, Texas: Lone Star, 1995. The first authoritative book published on soft-tip darts, including the lowdown on types of machines, how to play, and throwing techniques.

OTHER DARTS GAMES

Gotobed, Jabez. *Darts: Fifty Ways to Play the Game.* Oleander Press, 1980. This book includes a number of well-known alternative dart games, plus forty invented by the author, including one called "Marilyn Monroe."

Wellington, A. *The Various Dart Games and How to Play Them.* London: Universal Publications Ltd., 1937. A quick read for anyone eager to learn more about the darts "craze" that spread throughout England during the late 1930s.

PSYCHOLOGY

Duffy, Linda J., K. Anders Ericsson, and Bahman Baluch. "In Search of the Loci for Sex Differences in Throwing: The Effects of Physical Size and Differential Recruitment Rates on High Levels of Darts Performance." In *Research Quarterly for Exercise and Sport* 78, no. 1 (2007) pp. 71–78. One of the few academic articles used in the preparation of this book. Dr. Duffy and her colleagues lead the world in this type of research.

Low, Gary R. and Darwin B. Nelson. *Good Darts: Improving Your Game With Psychological and Self-Mastery Skills.* Corpus Christi, Texas: Good Darts Press, 1994. This interesting and unique work was the first attempt at applying psychology to the sport in book form.

WOMEN'S DARTS

Chaplin, Patrick. "[Women's] Darts." Karen Christensen, Allen Guttman, and Gertrud Pfister, eds., *International Encyclopedia of Women and Sports,* pp. 311–314. New York: Macmillan Reference, 2001. An interesting outline of the history and development of women's darts.

Dolowich, Madeline. *The Dart Book.* New York: Condor, 1978. To date the only darts "how-to" book written by a woman—and an American to boot! This was groundbreaking stuff three decades ago.

WEB SITES

American Darts Organization (ADO)—www.adodarts.com
Leading organization in the United States for steel-tip darts. Features rules, tournaments, and news.

British Darts Organisation (BDO)—www.bdodarts.com
The organization responsible for the development of darts in Britain since 1973. This site offers tournament news, BDO rules and regulations, and a news archive.

Bull's-Eye News (BEN)—www.bullseyenews.com
The top darts magazine for the United States and Canada featuring news, tournament updates and reports, and "Dartoid."

Darts History—www.patrickchaplin.com
Regarded by many as the foremost darts history Web site, the author's site also includes up-to-date news and some humor.

Dartoid (Paul Seigel)—www.dartoidsworld.com
One of the liveliest, most humorous, and often controversial Web sites, this site belongs to Paul Seigel, a syndicated darts journalist whose columns also appear in *Bull's-Eye News* (see above).

Darts World magazine—www.dartsworld.com
This magazine has been published in the UK since the fall of 1972 and continues today to record international darts news while also focusing on county results and performances.

Darts501.com–www.darts501.com
A comprehensive darts reference site.

National Darts Association—www.ndadarts.com
The sanctioning body of electronic darts in the United States.

Professional Darts Corporation (PDC)—www.pdc.tv.
This site features up-to-date news from the professional game and includes on-line match reports and videos and much more.

We Love Darts magazine—www.welovedarts.com
A new darts magazine launched in the UK in April 2009. It is a "glossy" featuring reports and articles from a number of respected contributors, including Eric Bristow and the author.

World Darts Federation (WDF)—www.dartswdf.com
This is the official Web site of the organization that coordinates darts across the world. Full of reports and tournament news, it is particularly useful for its links to all 60+ member nations.

APPENDIX E

The American Darts Organization (ADO) has granted permission for us to publish its rules as an Appendix to this book. The rules shown remain the copyright of the ADO and may not be copied or reproduced without the authority of the ADO.

TOURNAMENT RULES

Glossary of Terms

The following terms/meanings apply when used in the body of these Tournament Rules.

ADO: American Darts Organization

Bull: The center of the dartboard.

Chalker: Scorekeeper

Leg/Game: That element of a Match recognized as a fixed odd number, i.e., 301/501/701/1001 or Cricket

Hockey: A line or toe board marking the minimum throwing distance in front of the dartboard.

Masculine: Masculine gender nouns or pronouns include female

Match: The total number of Legs in the competition between two players/teams

Singular: Singular terms, where necessary, include the plural

Turn: A Turn consists of three darts, unless a Leg/Match is completed in a lesser amount.

Playing Rules

All darts events played under the exclusive supervision of and/or sanctioned by the ADO will be played in accordance with the following rules.

General

1. Good Sportsmanship will be the prevailing attitude throughout the tournament.

2. All players/teams will play by these Tournament Rules and, where necessary, any supplemental Rules stipulated by local Tournament Organizers.

3. The interpretation of these Tournament Rules, in relation to a specific darts event, will rest with local Tournament Organizers, whose decisions shall be final and binding. Protests after the fact will not be considered.

4. Any player/team who, during the course of any event, fails to comply with any of these Tournament Rules, will be subject to disqualification from that event.

5. Gambling is neither permitted nor sanctioned by the ADO.

6. The ADO will in the course of Tournament Sanctioning, ensure to the best of its ability, that the host/sponsor organization has the funding and/or sponsorship necessary to support the advertised cash prize structure for a darts event. The manner and matter of tournament prize payments are the responsibility of the respective host/sponsor organization and not that of the ADO.

7. The ADO assumes no responsibility for accident or injury on the premises.

8. The ADO reserves the right to add to or amend the ADO Tournament Rules at any time.

9. Decisions regarding the prize structure and event schedule, the method of player registration, and the choice of the match pairing system, are left at the discretion of local Tournament Organizers.

10. Each player is entitled to (9) NINE practice darts at the assigned matchboard prior to a match. No other practice darts may be thrown during the match without the permission of the chalker.

11. Tournament boards are reserved for assigned match pairings only. Boards are not to be used for practice, unless so designated by the Tournament Organizers.

12. Match pairings will be called three times only (minimum of 5 minutes between calls). Should a player/team fail to report to the assigned board within the 15 minutes allotted time, a Forfeit will be called. NOTE: Should a player/team be called to matches in two concurrent events (i.e., a female in both Women's only and an Open event), that player/team must choose in which event she/ they wish to continue play. A Forfeit will be called, unless that player/team can reach their assigned board within the 15 minutes.

13. Should a player's equipment become damaged, or be lost during the course of a turn, that player will be allowed up to a maximum of 5 minutes in which to repair/replace the playing equipment.

14. A maximum time limit of 5 minutes under exceptional circumstances, subject to the notification of the opponent and the chalker, will be allowed in the instance of a player requiring leaving the playing area during the course of match play.

15. Opponents and chalkers ONLY are allowed inside the playing area.

16. Opposing players must stand at least 2 feet behind the player at the hockey.

17. Should a player have any portion of his feet or shoes over the hockey line during a turn, all darts so thrown will be counted as part of his turn, but any score made by said darts will be invalid and not counted. One warning by a tournament official will be considered sufficient before invoking this rule.

18. A player wishing to throw a dart, or darts, from a point either side of the hockey must keep his feet behind an imaginary straight line extending from either side of the hockey.

Turn

19. A Turn consists of three darts, unless a Leg/Match is completed in a lesser amount.

20. All darts must be thrown by, and from, the hand. The player is allowed a total of 3 minutes to complete their turn as timed by a tournament official. No darts will be allowed to be thrown after 3 minutes.

21. Should a player "touch" any dart that is in the dartboard during a turn, that turn will be deemed to have been completed.

22. A dart bouncing off or falling out of the dartboard will not be rethrown.

Starting and Finishing (All Events)

The tournament director will have the option of a draw, a toss of a coin, or a throw for the bull to determine the order of play in each match.

If a throw for the bull is used, rules #23, 24, and 25 apply.

23. All Matches will begin with a coin flip to determine who has the option to throw 1st or 2nd at the Inner Bull. The player throwing closest to the Inner Bull will throw first in the 1st Leg. The Loser of the 1st Leg has the option of throwing for the Inner Bull first in the 2nd Leg. If the 3rd Leg is necessary, the Inner Bull will again be thrown, with the loser of the original coin flip having the option of throwing first.

24. The second thrower may acknowledge the first dart as an Inner or Outer Bull and ask for that dart to be removed prior to his throw. Should the first dart be removed without the request of the 2nd thrower, a rethrow will occur; with the 2nd thrower now having the option of throwing first. The dart must remain in the board in order to count. Additional throws may be made, until the player's dart remains in the board. Should the 2nd thrower dislodge the dart of the 1st, a rethrow will be made with the 2nd thrower now throwing first. Rethrows shall be called if the chalker cannot decide which dart is closest to the Inner Bull, or if both darts are anywhere in the Inner Bull, or both darts are anywhere in the Outer Bull. The decision of the chalker is final. Should a rethrow be necessary, the darts will be removed and the person who threw 2nd will now throw 1st.

25. For the purpose of starting and finishing a Leg/Match, the Inner Bull is considered a double 25.

    If a drawer or a toss of a coin is used, the following should apply:

26. The winner of the drawer or toss shall throw first in the match. If the match is divided into legs, the winner of the drawer or toss shall throw first in the odd-numbered legs, and the loser shall throw first in the even-numbered legs.

27. If the match is divided into sets, then the winner of the draw or toss shall throw first in the odd-numbered legs of the odd-numbered sets, and first in the even-numbered legs in the even-numbered sets, with the loser throwing first in the other legs.

28. In the instance of a match that is divided into legs, being equal before the start of the deciding leg, then the throwing order of the deciding leg shall be decided by throwing for the bull. The procedure at this point shall be as set down in rules 23–25.

29. In the instance of a match that is divided into sets, being equal before the start of the deciding set, then the throwing order for the deciding set shall be decided by throwing for the bull. The procedure at this point shall be as set down in rules 23–25.

30. In those tournaments where a Tie-Breaker Rule is applicable, then the proceeding two paragraphs shall not supercede the rule.

(DOUBLE/TEAM EVENTS)

31. It is permissible for the Doubles/Team player finishing a Leg, to throw for the Inner Bull and start the subsequent Leg. It is also permissible for one member of a Doubles or Team to throw for the Inner Bull 1st, and have his partner or teammate shoot first in the leg.

32. It is permissible for a Double or Team to participate with fewer than the required number of players, provided that the team forfeits a turn(s) in each rotation, equal to the number of missing players. The missing player(s) may NOT join a Leg in progress, but is allowed to participate in a subsequent Leg(s) of that Match.

33. At the tournament director's discretion, women may be recycled in mixed doubles and triples events only.

34. No substitutes will be allowed after the first round of Doubles/Team play.

SCORING

35. A scoreboard must be mounted within 4' laterally from the dartboard and at not more than a 45-degree angle from the dartboard. It must be clearly visible in front of the player at the hockey.

36. In all ADO sanctioned tournaments, you must have a chalker if one is available. If one is not available, the player must leave the darts in the board until the score is recorded.

37. The chalker will mark the scores made in the outer columns of the scoreboard, and the totals remaining in the two middle columns.

38. The chalker, if asked, may inform the thrower what he has scored and/or what he has left. He MAY NOT inform the thrower what he has left in terms of number combinations. It IS permissible for a partner, teammate, or a spectator to advise the thrower during the course of a Match. See #1.

39. No one, including the thrower or chalker, should touch the darts prior to the decision of the chalker.

40. For a dart to score, it must remain in the board 5 seconds after the 3rd or final dart has been thrown by that player. The tip of the dart point must be touching the bristle portion of the board.

41. A dart's score shall be determined from the side of the wire at which the point of the dart enters the wire segment.

42. Should a dart lodge directly between the connecting wires on the dartboard, making it impossible to determine on which side of the wire the dart resides, the score shall always be the higher value of the two segments in question. This includes the outside double ring for the game shot. Determination as to whether the dart is directly between the wires will be made in accordance with rules #39 and #41.

43. It is the responsibility of the player to verify his score before removing his darts from the board. The score remains as written if one or more darts has been removed.

44. In Doubles/Team events, no player may throw (during a Leg) until each of his teammates has completed his turn. The FIRST player throwing out of turn will receive a score of zero points for that round and his Team will forfeit the turn.

45. Errors in arithmetic stand as written, unless corrected prior to the beginning of that player's next turn. In case of Doubles/Team matches, such errors must be rectified prior to the next turn of any partner/player on that team.

46. A Leg/Match is concluded at such time as a player/team hits the "double" required to reduce their remaining score to zero, unless otherwise stated by the local Tournament Organizers. All darts thrown subsequently will not count for score.

47. The "BUST RULE" will apply. If the player scores one less, equal, or more points than needed to reach zero, he has "busted." His score reverts to the score required prior to the beginning of his turn.

48. Fast finishes such as 3 in a bed, 222, 111, Shanghai, etc., do not apply.

ADDITIONAL ADO AMERICAN CRICKET RULES

The following rules shall apply for ADO Sanctioned Cricket events, effective January 1, 1984.

49. Cricket is played using the numbers 20, 19, 18, 17, 16, 15 and both the Inner and Outer Bull.

50. To close a number, the player/team must score three of that number. The double and triple ring count as 2 or 3, respectively. Closure can be accomplished with three singles, a single and a double, or a triple.

51. Once a player/team closes a number, he/they may score points on that number until the opponent also closes that number. The double and triple count as 2 or 3 times the numerical values, respectively. All numerical scores are added to the previous balance. Once both players/teams have scored three of a number, it is "closed," and no further scoring can be made on that number by either player/team.

52. To close the bull, the Outer Bull counts as a single, and the Inner Bull counts as a double.

53. Numbers can be "owned" or "closed" in any order desired by the individual player/team. Calling your shot is not required.

54. It shall be the responsibility of the player to verify his score before removing his darts from the board. The score remains as written if one or more darts has been removed from the board. In accordance with the inherent "strategy" involved in the Cricket game, corrections in arithmetic must be made before the next player throws. See #1.

55. Winning the game:

- The player/team that closes all the numbers first and has the highest numerical score will be declared the winner.

- If both sides are tied in points, or have no points, the first player/team to close the specified numbers will be the winner.

- If a player/team closes the numbers first, and is behind in points, he/they must continue to score on any number not closed until either the point deficit is made up or the opponent has closed all the numbers.

EQUIPMENT

DARTS

56. Darts used in tournament play cannot exceed an overall maximum length of 30.5 cm (12 in.), nor weigh more than 50 gm per dart. Each dart will consist of a recognizable point, barrel, and flight.

DARTBOARD

57. The dartboard will be a standard 18" bristle board, of the type approved by the ADO, and will be of the standard 1–20 clock pattern. A scoreboard is necessary, see rule #35.

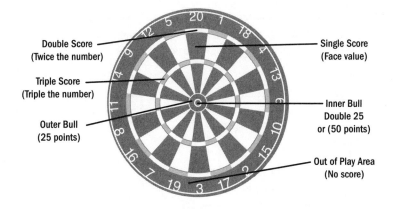

Double Score
(Twice the number)

Triple Score
(Triple the number)

Outer Bull
(25 points)

Single Score
(Face value)

Inner Bull
Double 25
or (50 points)

Out of Play Area
(No score)

STANDARD DIMENSIONS

Double and Triple rings inside width measurement = 8 mm (5⁄16")

Inner Bull inside diameter = 12.7 mm (0.5")

Outer Bull inside diameter = 31 mm (1.25")

Outside edge of Double wire to Inner Bull = 170 mm (6.75")

Outside edge of Triple wire to Inner Bull = 117mm (4.25")

Outside edge of Double wire to outside edge of Double wire = 342 mm (13.5")

Overall dartboard diameter = 457 mm (18.0")

Spider wire gauge (Maximum Standard Wire Gauge) = 16 SWG

58. The scoring wedge indicated by 20 will be the darker of the two
wedge colors and must be at the top center wedge.

59. No alterations/accessories may be added to the board setups.

60. The inner narrow band will score "Triple" the segment number
and the outer narrow band will score "Double" the segment number.

61. The outer center ring (Outer Bull) is scored at "25" and the inner
center ring (Inner Bull) is scored at "50."

62. The minimum throwing distance is 7' 9¼". The board height is 5' 8" (floor to the center of the Inner Bull; 9' 7⅜" measured diagonally from the Inner Bull to the back of the raised hockey at floor level).

Lighting

63. Lights must be affixed in such a way as to brightly illuminate the board, reduce to a minimum the shadows cast by the darts, and not physically impede the flight of a dart.

Hockey

64. Whenever possible, a raised hockey, at least 1½" high and 2' long, will be placed in position at the minimum throwing distance, and will measure from the back of the raised hockey 7' 9¼" along the floor to a plumb line at the face of the dartboard.

65. In the event the hockey is a tape or similar "flush" marking, the minimum throwing distance is measured from the front edge of the tape closest to the dartboard.

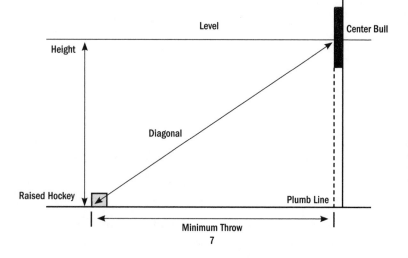

7

Inner Bull Height = 1.73 meters (5' 8")

Minimum Throwing Distance = 2.37 meters (7' 9¼")

Diagonal–Inner Bull to back of hockey = 2.93 meters (9' 7⅜")

Height of raised hockey = 33 mm (1½")

Length of raised hockey = 610 mm (2' 0")

Conversion Factor

Diagonal Length = $\sqrt{\text{Height}^2 + \text{Hockey}^2}$

$$= \sqrt{1.73^2 + 2.37^2}$$

$$= \sqrt{2.9929 + 5.6169}$$

$$= \sqrt{8.6098}$$

$$= 2.934 \text{ meters (9' 7⅜")}$$

APPENDIX F

ABBREVIATIONS

ADO	American Darts Organization
BDO	British Darts Organisation
NAODT	North American Open Dart Tournament
NDA	National Darts Association (England 1925–1939)
NDA	National Darts Association (United States soft-tip association)
PDC	Professional Darts Corporation
SCDA	Southern California Darts Association
USDA	United States Darting Association
WDC	World Darts Council
WDF	World Darts Federation

ILLUSTRATION CREDITS
Figures 1–4, 7, 8, 10, 14, and 15: Chris Barrell
Figures 5, 9, and 11–13: David King
Figures 6, 16: Nodor International Ltd.

INDEX

"Addagram," 141

"Against the darts," definition of, 148

Alcohol and darts, 94

American Darts Organization
abbreviation for, 176
"bust rule," 35
rules, 164–175
Web site, 162

Anderson, Bob, 82, 134

Arrows, definition of, 148

Bag o' nuts, definition of, 148

Barneveld, Raymond van
biographical information about, 125
and 2007 world title, 142
and use of earplugs, 141

Barrels, 16, 17, 148

Barrett, Tom, stance of, 23

Baseball, 49, 50, 51

Basement, definition of, 148

Basic dart training, 83, 84

Bed, definition of, 148

Bed and breakfast, definition of, 149

Beehives, definition of, 149

"Best Foot Forward," 22

Blind killer, 75, 76

"Bogey numbers"
definition of, 149
and 501, 34
and outshots, 37

"Bounce-outs"
causes of, 93, 94
and damaged dart points, 16
definition of, 149
occasional, 89

Brackin, Ivan, 86, 159

"Breaking the serve," 32

"Bristle" dartboard, 7

Bristow, Eric
biographical information about, 125, 126
and dartitis, 98, 99
and darts averages, 39
darts grip of, 20, 21
and second British darts boom, 106
stance of, 23

British Darts Organisation
abbreviation for, 176
and drug testing, 95
and first-ever Women's World Darts Championship, 117
and formal structure for progression, 114
formation of, 106
Web site, 162
and women's darts, 116

Bromberg, Stacy, 126, 127

Brush, definition of, 149

Bucci, Timothy R., 110, 160

"Bull," 72

"Bulling-up," 32, 149

Bull's-eye
definition of, 149
location of, 10
use of term, ix

Bust (ed), definition of, 149

"Busting" his score, 34, 35

"Bust" rule, 34, 35

"Caller," 140, 149

Carver, Ray, 132

"Chalker"
definition of, 149
in English cricket, 53

in soft-tip darts, 140

Chaplin, Patrick, 157, 161, 180

Check out, definition of, 150

Check-out tables, 139

"Chucker," definition of, 150

Circumluminator, 15

Clickety click, definition of, 150

"Closing" numbers, 40

Come out, definition of, 150

Compass points, 62

Cork, definition of, 150. See also Bull's-eye.

"Cover shot," 29, 150

"Crawling around," 72

Cribbage, 30, 31

Cricket, 39, 40–47

Croft, Olly, 105, 106

Crowds and darts, 97

Dart, Oxford English Dictionary definition of, 100

Dartboards
caring for and maintaining, 18
construction of, 7, 172
customized, 142
dimensions of, 9, 10, 173, 174
origin of, 5, 6
positioning, 13
setting up, 12, 13
standardized, 6

Dartitis
definition of, 150
description of, 98, 99
and Eric Bristow, 126

"Darts court," 12, 150

Darts (equipment)
addagram, 4

Darts (continued)
  area for, 11, 12
  barrels, first brass, 3, 4
  cabinets for, 12, 13
  caring for and maintaining,
    16
  check-out tables, 139, 140
  earplugs, 141
  evolution of, 2
  flights, 137, 138, 142
  gripping, 19, 20, 21
  mats for, 13
  nonslip finger wax, 139
  parts of, 7, 8, 9
  scorers, 140
  shafts, 138, 139, 142
  sharpeners for, 16
  tungsten, 4, 5
  wallet and cases, 140, 141
  weights of, 8, 9
Darts (playing)
  averages, 39
  baseball (game), 49, 50, 51
  basics of, 19–29
  biographies and
    autobiographies, 157
  blind killer (game), 75, 76
  bowls (game), 51, 52
  clothing when playing, 24, 25
  compass points (game), 62
  cricket (game), 40–47
  doubles killer (game), 63, 64
  double ya! (game), 79
  English cricket (game), 52,
    53–54
  equipment for, 1–18
  etiquette, 111, 112, 159, 160
  51 (game), 84, 85
  fives (game), 66, 67
  501 (game), 30, 32–37
  fox and hound (game), 67, 68
  grip, 19, 20, 21

halve it (game), 68, 69, 70
high and low boxes (game),
  60, 61, 62
history of, books on, 157, 158
history of, Web site, 162
hit the dollar (game), 76
humor, books on, 160
improving, 80–92
instruction, 159, 160
and lighting, 14
little and large (game), 64,
  65, 66
mathematics, 80, 81, 82
middle for diddle (game),
  85
1,001 (game), 70, 71, 72
perfect game, 38
as popular sport and
  recreational activity, viii
psychology of, information
  on, 161
referee, 113
rewards (game), 86
round the clock (game), 72
and safety techniques, 93, 94
scram (game), 72, 73
shanghai (game), 73, 74, 75,
  78, 79
shove ha' penny (game), 58,
  59, 60
soccer (game), 55
soft-tip, books on, 161
stance, 21, 22–23, 24
straight-in 101 (game), 85
ten up (game), 85, 86
tic-tac-toe (game), 55, 56–57,
  58, 76, 77, 78
throw, 26, 27, 28
women's, information
  about, 162
Web sites, information
  about, 162–163

Darts playing legends
  Barneveld, Raymond van,
    125
  Bristow, Eric, 125, 126
  Bromberg, Stacy, 126, 127
  David, Tony, 127
  Dobromyslova, Anastasia,
    128
  Flowers, Mauren, 128, 129
  George, Bobby, 129
  Gulliver, Trina, 129, 130
  Hedman, Deta, 130, 131
  Hoenselaar, Francis, 131
  Kuczynski, Johnny, 132
  Lowe, John, 132, 133
  Part, John, 133
  Rees, Leighton, 133, 134
  Taylor, Phil, 134, 135
  Wade, James, 135
  Wilson, Jocky, 136
Darts Regulation Authority,
  and drug testing, 95
Darts Scores for Charity
  Foundation, 127
Darts World magazine
  and coining of word "dartitis,"
    98
  and national darts
    tournaments, 119
  Web site, 162
David, Tony, 127
Dedication when playing
  darts, 90, 91
Deller, Keith, 28, 126
Dirty darts, definition of, 150
Dobromyslova, Anastasia,
  117, 128
Double, definition of, 150
Double bull, definition of, 150
Double in, definition of, 150
"Double in, double out" rule, 33
Double out, definition of, 151

Doubles killer (game), 63, 64
Double top, 83, 151
Double trouble, definition of, 151
"Drawing room archery," 101
Drugs and darts, 95
Duffy, Linda, 118, 161

Earplugs, 141
Eating and darts, 95
Edwards, Rhian, 130
Eights, definition of, 151
Electronic darts. *See* Soft-tip darts.
Elliott, Maurice, 109
Embassy World Professional Darts Championships, 125, 126, 127, 129, 130, 132, 133, 134, 136
England, darts in
Annakin case, 102
during World World I, 103
first darts boom, 104, 105
and formation of National Darts Association, 103, 104
and "London" game, 104
in the nineteenth century, 100, 101
origins of modern game, 101, 102
second darts boom, 105, 106, 107
English cricket, 52, 53–54
Exhibition, definition of, 151

Fallout, definition of, 151
Fat, definition of, 151
Feathers, definition of, 151
Finger grip wax, 21, 139
Finishing double, definition of, 151

Fitness and health (when playing darts), 91
"50." *See* Bull's-eye.
501, 30, 32–37
"Five times round," 15
Fives, 66, 67, 151
Flechettes, 101
"Flighting" darts, 20
Flights
cardboard, 4
caring for and maintaining, 17
definition of, 151
feather, 4
protector for, 138
shapes of, 137, 138
types of, 138
Flowers, Maureen, 128, 129
Follow on. *See* Little and large
Formal rules for darts, 92
Foul dart, 41
Fox and hound, 67, 68
"French darts," 2, 3, 138
Fritzgerald, William, 86, 159

Game on, definition of, 151
Game-shot, definition of, 151
Gamesmanship, 96, 97
Gamlin, Brian, 101, 102
Garden gates, definition of, 151
Garside, James, 102
George, Bobby, 33, 129
Get the odd off, definition of, 151
Good group, definition of, 152
Gulliver, Trina
autobiography of, 158
biographical information about, 129, 130

and first-ever Women's Darts Championship, 117
and match versus Anastasia Dobromyslova, 128

Halve it, 68, 69, 70
Hedman, Deta, 130, 131
High and low boxes, 60, 61, 62
Hit the dollar, 76
Hockey, definition of, 152
Hoenselaar, Francis, 117, 131
"Home of Darts," 123
"House darts," 5, 152
House rules, definition of, 152

"Indoor quoits." *See* Rings.
Inner bull, definition of, 152

Javelot, 101
"Jocky Wilson Cup," 136
Killer. *See* Doubles killer
King, David, 37
King, Gale, 116
King George VI, 104, 105, 116
Kuczynski, Johnny, 132

Ladbrokes.com World Darts Championship, 125
Lakeside World Professional Darts Championship. *See also* Embassy World Professional Darts Championships
and broadcasted BDO events, 107
origin of, 122
and women's darts, 116, 118
"Last scoring dart rule," 35
"Leg," definition of, 120, 152
Level pegging, definition of, 152
Lim, Paul, 38

Little and large, 64, 65, 66
"Loading," 2, 3
Loop, 152
Lowe, John
  autobiography of, 158
  biographical information
    about, 132, 133
  book on darts instruction
    and etiquette, 159
  and darts averages, 39
  and nine-dart finish, 38
  and second British darts
    boom, 158

"Madhouse," 83, 152
"Markers," 140
Married man's side, definition
  of, 152
Mathematics of darts, 80, 81,
  82
Maximum, definition of, 152
McClintock, Jack, 157
Mickey Mouse. *See* cricket
Middle for diddle, 85, 150
"Mixed laterals," 28
"Mugs away," 34, 152

National Darts Association
  abbreviation for, 176
  formation of, 103, 104
  Web site, 163
Nearest and farthest, definition
  of, 153
Nerves when playing darts, 89
News of the World
  darts competition, 1979,
    128
  darts competition, and
    women players, 115
  and first darts boom, 104,105
Nine dart perfect game, 38,
  153

Nines, definition of, 153
No bust, definition of, 153
Nodor, 7

Oche
  conforming to current dart
    rules, 11
  definition of, 153
  measuring, 14
  movement along the, 28, 29
  use of term, ix
"Off the island," 11, 54, 153
Old hens, definition of, 153
01 games, origins of, 30, 31
1,001, 70, 71, 72
"Outer bull," 10, 140
Outshots
  chart, 146–147
  definition of, 153
  using to complete game of
    501, 36, 37
"Owning" numbers, 40

Part, John, 133
Pearson, John, 108
Peek, Dan, 107, 108, 157
Perfect game of darts, 38, 158
Pie, definition of, 153
"Point monger," 42, 153
Points, 16, 17
Potter, Stephen, 96
Practice games
  51, 84
  middle for diddle, 85
  rewards, 86
  straight-in 101, 85
  ten up, 85, 86
Practicing darts, 82, 83–86,
  87
Priestley, Dennis, 124
Professional Darts Corporation
  abbreviation for, 176

creation of, 106, 107, 123,
  124
  and "Jocky Wilson Cup," 136
  tournaments, and "bulling-
    up," 32
  Web site, 163
Proficiency at darts, 87
Psychology of darts, articles
  on, 161
"Puff and dart," 2, 101

Queen Elizabeth, 104, 105,
  116

Ranking event, definition of,
  153
"Red bit," 18, 33, 153
Rees, Leighton
  biographical information
    about, 133, 134
  and second British darts
    boom, 106
  and women darts
    champions, 117, 118
"Regional dartboards," 6
Rewards, 86
Rings, 103
Right there, definition of, 154
Rituals when playing darts, 90
Robin Hood, definition of,
  154
Round the clock, 72
"Round of nine," 41, 154
Route 66, 154

Safety techniques when
  playing darts, 93, 94
Scoreboard, electronic, 13
"Scorer," 72, 73, 140
Scram, 72, 73
Segment, definition of, 154
Set, definition of, 154

Sevens, definition of, 154
Shafts
    caring for and maintaining, 17
    definition of, 154
    types of, 138, 139
Shanghai, 73, 74, 75, 154
Shooter, definition of, 154
Shove ha' penny, 58, 59, 60
"Side-footed stance," 22, 23
Silly shanghai, 78
Silly tic-tac-toe, 76, 77, 78
Singles, Doubles, and Triples Combination Chart, 36, 145
Sixes, definition of, 154
Smoking and darts, 95
Soccer (football), 54
Soft-tip darts
    books about, 161
    history of, 109, 110
    weight of, 9
"Spider," 11, 154
Splash, definition of, 154
Split, definition of, 154, 155
Split the number, definition of, 155
"Splitting" a number, 35
Standard dart grip, 19, 20
Staying cool when playing darts, 97, 98
"Stems." See shafts.
Stoddart, Graeme, 116
"Stopper," 72, 73
"Straight in
    definition of, 155
    501, 33, 34
    101, 85
Strutt, Joseph, 100, 101
Sunset Strip, definition of, 155

Tactics. See cricket
Take chalks, definition of, 155

"Take the odd off," 82
"Taking the darts," 32
Taylor, Phil
    autobiography of, 158
    biographical information about, 134, 135
    and darts averages, 39
    and first WDC World Championship, 124
    and match versus Johnny Kuczynski, 132
    and match versus Raymond van Barneveld, 125, 132
    and 2007 world title, 143
Temperament when playing darts, 89, 90
Ten up, 85, 86
"Third dart syndrome," 28
Three in a bed, definition of, 155
"Three times round," 15
Throw line, ix, 155. See also Oche
Tic-tac-toe, 55, 56–57, 58
"Toe-line." See Oche
Ton, definition of, 155
Tournaments, information about, 119
Triple, definition of, 155
Trombones, definition of, 155
"Tungstens," 4, 5
Turn, definition of, 155
"25." See Outer bull
"Twice round," 15
Two trees, definition of, 155

United States, darts in the
    growth of, 108, 109
    legends, 126, 127, 132
    myths about Pilgrims, 107
    origins of, 107, 108

Waddell, Sid, 134
Wade, James, 135
Wallet and cases (for darts), 140, 141
Warne, Baden, 109
Wedge. See Pie
Wet feet, definition of, 156
White horse, definition of, 156
Williamson, Noel E., 36, 85
Wilson, Jocky
    biographical information about, 136
    and second British darts boom, 106
WINMAU World Masters
    and broadcasted BDO events, 107
    description of, 122, 123
    1991, 128
    and women's darts, 116, 118
"With the darts," 148
Women's darts. See also Darts legends
    books about, 162
    future of, 117, 118
    history of, 115, 116, 117
Wood, Tony, 98
World Darts Council
    abbreviation for, 176
    in the 1990s, 106, 107
    and the 16 "rebel" darts players, 123, 124
World Darts Federation
    abbreviation for, 176
    establishment of, 106
    Web site, 163
Wrong bed, definition of, 156

X, definition of, 156

ABOUT THE AUTHOR

DR. PATRICK CHAPLIN has played darts in numerous pubs and clubs across Britain for more than forty years and has won several trophies. However, while not professing to ever being (or likely ever becoming) a great darts player, he does have extensive knowledge of the sport and is recognized throughout the world as a foremost authority on the history of the game.

Patrick has written extensively on darts in the UK for *Darts World* and *We Love Darts* magazines and numerous other British publications. Each year many thousands of fans visit his darts Web site (www.patrickchaplin. com) to learn of his latest discoveries. In 2006, Patrick's lifetime of research culminated in the award of a PhD in the social history of darts by the Anglia Ruskin University, Cambridge, England. His dissertation, *Darts in England 1900–1939: A Social History,* was published by the Manchester University Press in 2009. For this reason, Patrick is now popularly known as "Dr. Darts."

He has also coauthored two major darts autobiographies, John Lowe's *Old Stoneface* (2005) and Trina Gulliver's *Golden Girl* (2008).

Patrick lives in Essex, England, with his wife, Maureen, and their cat, Angel. They are within 500 yards of a pub dartboard.